# THE PRADO

# THE
# PRADO

F. J. SÁNCHEZ CANTÓN

FORMER DIRECTOR
OF THE PRADO MUSEUM

LONDON
THAMES AND HUDSON

TRANSLATED FROM THE FRENCH
BY JAMES CLEUGH

*First published in Great Britain in 1959*
*This new revised edition 1971*
*Fifth printing*

© THAMES AND HUDSON LTD, LONDON 1959 AND 1971

THIS BOOK IS PUBLISHED IN FRANCE BY EDITIONS AIMERY SOMOGY, PARIS

*Printed in West Germany by K.G. Lohse, Frankfurt am Main*

ISBN 0 500 18123 3 clothbound
ISBN 0 500 20117 X paperback

# CONTENTS

# FOREWORD

The agitation aroused throughout the world by the news during the Civil War that the Prado was threatened gave an indication of the importance to the very existence of our civilization of the preservation of its masterpieces. From all parts of the world visitors came like pilgrims to the unforgettable exhibition of the treasures of the museum held in 1939 at Geneva. Later, during the War, monuments and museums all over Europe found themselves in the same danger, and the protective measures which this first alarm had necessitated proved of great value. There were to be many more migrations of master-pieces, many more itinerant exhibitions before the treasures of Europe resumed their positions in their old homes. However, the interval had given an opportunity for many of the museums to be renovated, enlarged and improved.

There are few better ways of going back to the very sources of European culture than to retrace the history of these great institutions, for they preserve the essence of man's creative genius. This is all the more true in that each great museum has an individual character: the various elements that go to make up each one bear witness to the spirit and mentality of the men who brought them together.

Of the Prado, I would say only that it is a museum which lends itself exceptionally well to contemplation and study, for it is organized with the public in mind. This is not nearly as common as may be imagined and one may perhaps see in it a manifestation of Spanish generosity and nobility of spirit. With a conscientiousness fairly rare at the present time, when so many take it upon themselves to impose on others their own preferences and prejudices, the curators of the Prado make it their aim to exhibit all the works in their care. The basic principle of their method of presentation is objectivity and they subordinate their personal tastes to the demands of history and scholarship. The fact that every room of the museum is open every day without exception, that there are always the best possible facilities for working, photographing and copying, is of the greatest importance to the Prado's visitors who have often come from a considerable distance and who consequently appreciate these advantages at their full value. And if one remembers that during the recent regrouping of Goya's work and the extension of the galleries devoted to El Greco and the great Flemish and Venetian masters there was no restriction of entry to the museum, it can be seen that the curators of the Prado are capable of real *tours de force*.

A large share of the credit for this efficiency must go to F. J. Sánchez Cantón who for many decades has been closely connected with the life of the great Spanish museum, its acquisitions, improvement and installations. Nobody is better qualified to tell the history of its collections and to pay homage to those who amassed them, to the monarchs distinguished for their pioneering spirit, such as Isabella the Catholic, Charles V, and Philip II, as to less fortunate monarchs who nevertheless deserve our gratitude for their patronage. In the final analysis, which is the better claim to fame: to have deserved the friendship of Velasquez or to have encouraged the first steps of Goya?

This book includes colour-reproductions of all the principal masterpieces of the Prado; their value is increased by the solid, dispassionate scholarship with which the author describes them and gives the latest findings of research on each individual point. The pictures in Madrid have benefited from exceptionally good climatic conditions and have been subjected to a minimum of handling and cleaning. They remain as nearly as possible in the state in which they were created. A knowledge of them is indispensable for any student of Spanish art, or indeed of the Flemish or Venetian schools.

This incomparable museum contains all the important works by Velasquez as well as examples of the convolutions of Goya's thought; it is the museum richest in works by Hieronymus Bosch, Patinir and Titian; its collections of Tintoretto, Veronese, Rubens and van Dyck are superb, while it possesses outstanding examples of the Master of Flémalle, Rogier van der Weyden, Brueghel, Raphael and Mantegna. Its new El Greco rooms, with their carefully planned acquisitions, now comprise the most complete representation of this painter. This book will undoubtedly be the introduction to an unforgettable visit, under the aegis of the best possible guide.

JACQUES LASSAIGNE

THE COLLECTIONS OF THE KINGS OF SPAIN

THE PRADO is one of the most famous galleries in existence. It also offers more unprecedented features than any other in the circumstances of its origin and history. It is unique for a number of different reasons. The collection was formed by discriminating and knowledgeable royal patrons whose perseverance was never equalled. Their tastes are reflected in the items selected. The pictures are in a fine state of preservation. Finally, the chances and changes of the Museum's most recent history have been followed with the deepest interest throughout the world.

The study of this collection requires, far more than in the case of other galleries, a preliminary acquaintance with its past, which throws a flood of light on the whole subject.


*The Earliest Acquisitions*

Beginning in the reign of John II, who died in 1445, the kings of Spain, or rather, at that time, of Castile, showed themselves to be generous patrons of painting. They were not the only kings to be so. But it is a remarkable fact that in Spain artistic tastes were regularly transmitted to the successive occupants of the throne, even when the dynasty changed. The family of Transtamare, the house of Austria and the Bourbons all maintained this tradition. It is true that some of the sovereigns in question lacked both high intelligence and refined culture, as did, for instance, Charles II, Charles IV, Ferdinand VII and Isabella II. But even these monarchs took a lively interest in painting. Nowhere else in Europe were such tastes prolonged for three centuries. They enabled a wonderful collection of works of art, chosen with incomparable discrimination, to be assembled at the Prado.

Before entering upon an outline of the Museum's history, comprising its foundation, methods of management and the various royal contributions to its establishment, I should like to point out another outstanding fact in relation to the collection. None of its masterpieces was acquired by war or violence. The kings of Spain controlled a vast extent of territories in Europe, containing great quantities of the pictures of which they were so fond. Yet they always respected, throughout the different countries they governed, the property of churches and monasteries and that of individuals. If circumstances permitted, they acquired the works they admired by purchase. Otherwise they had the paintings copied.

The present wonderful display at the Prado has not reached modern times without serious loss. Damage was sustained by the royal collections in four fires, of which two were particularly destructive. There were outbreaks of fire at the Prado Palace on 11 March 1604, at the Escorial in 1671 and 1763 and at the Alcazar, which suffered badly, on 24 December 1734. Further disasters occurred during the Wars of the Succession (1710) and against Napoleon (1808–1813). Thefts were committed and hardly any attempt was made to recover the portions of 'King Joseph's luggage' which had fallen into the hands of Wellington. It will therefore be readily understood that by the nineteenth century the treasures of the royal collections had been appreciably reduced.

But what was left remains in a perfect state of preservation. The truth of this statement can be proved, for example, by the condition of the Poussins at the Prado as compared with those in other galleries. The dry, uncontaminated air of the Castilian table-land, the immobility for centuries, or at least the short duration of the moves made, of the panels and canvases, together with the smallest possible resort to chemical methods in the conservation and cleaning of the pictures, a traditional precaution of the Court Painters to whom such tasks were assigned and still observed by the Prado officials, all contributed to maintain the collection in its unique freedom from deterioration.

The first royal acquisitions antedate the middle of the fifteenth century. At that period John II possessed three panels by 'Master Rogier van der Weyden, the great and famous Fleming', which he offered to the Carthusian monastery of Miraflores at Burgos. These panels are today in the Berlin Museum. This isolated evidence does no more than suggest the existence of a royal collection, such as

*Isabella the Catholic*

was definitely established in the reign of Queen Isabella the Catholic (1473–1504).

She assembled whole sets of pictures, of which the inventories still exist. Over fifty of these paintings have survived. Thirty-eight are in the Royal Chapel at Granada, fifteen in the Royal Palace at Madrid and a dozen in various collections abroad. There are therefore no works in the Prado which are known for certain to have belonged to her. It is believed, nevertheless, that a certain panel, originally in the church of Santo Tomas at Avila, was ordered by Queen Isabella. It represents her in prayer at the feet of the Virgin and Child, accompanied by her husband, by Prince Juan and Princess Isabel, by Father Tomas de Torquemada and by Pedro Martir de Anghiera (or Angliera), author of *Orbe Novo Decades,* the first history of America.

A large proportion of Isabella's collection was sold at her death, including the forty-seven panels of the polyptych executed by Juan de Flandes and Miguel Sitium. Fifteen of these were recovered. The other thirty-two had been acquired by Margaret of Austria, Isabella's daughter-in-law. The pictures presented to the Chapel Royal at Granada were not included in the sale. The surviving works formerly in the great Queen's collection show her preference for Flemish artists. The only Italian paintings among them are Botticelli's *Agony in the Garden* and Perugino's *Resurrection.*

During the short reign of Philip the Handsome and the minority of Charles V not much interest was taken in pictures. Charles' mother, the unfortunate Joanna the Mad, Queen of Castile, possessed only a few works. The inventory taken at her death in 1555 notes some twenty-three items, comprising altarpieces and devotional paintings, some with French inscriptions, and four portraits, those of Isabella the Catholic and her daughters.


*Charles V*


As soon as the future Emperor Charles V was in a position to give free rein to the amazing vitality that characterized his whole life, he showed a decided taste for the arts and in particular for painting. Beroqui writes: 'The fact is attested by his visits to Bologna and the advice he later gave to Francis of Holland not to miss seeing

TITIAN *Charles V on Horseback at Mühlberg.* Detail

the pictures in the church of St Michael in that city. At Augsburg the only member of the Lutheran suite of his prisoner John Frederick of Saxony whom Charles received graciously was Cranach the Elder, who had painted his portrait when he was a child. The artist told the Emperor that the only object which would make the little prince look up and keep still for a moment was a lance. Charles's tastes were fastidious. He admired Correggio and Parmigianino. But his favourite was Titian. He insisted on the painter coming to Spain and accompanying him on his military expedition to Tunis.

An inventory of the pictures which the Emperor brought back to Spain was signed at Brussels on 18 August 1556. It included Titian's *Holy Trinity* or '*La Gloria*', his *Ecce Homo* and *Mater Dolorosa*, his portraits of the Emperor and Empress, of the Empress alone and of Charles in armour, as well as several religious compositions by Coxcie and Moro's portrait of Mary Tudor.

Several paintings from Charles's collection are today at the Prado, such as the triptych by Memling and Jacopo Bassano's *Animals boarding the Ark* and others.

The second inventory of the Emperor's property was drawn up at the castle of Simancas on 26 February 1561. It includes pictures inherited from Joanna the Mad, together with the *Annunciation* of Titian, a portrait by the same artist on wood and six other portraits, on canvas, of the wife and five daughters of Ferdinand, King of the Romans. All these works, with few exceptions, are of rare quality.


*Philip II*


Studies of the personality of the son of Charles V are seldom comprehensive enough. His political ideas are still hotly debated, of course. But all too often his great interest in art is forgotten. His accession marks a most important date in the history of the patrons of artists. For King Philip not only loved painting for its own sake, commissioning and purchasing works of great merit, but also proved himself a true connoisseur. Passages in his correspondence, for in-

TITIAN *Self-portrait*

*Maria of Hungary*

stance, show him even to have been anxious about the packing of pictures to be despatched to him from Venice.

He first met Titian at Milan between 20 December 1548 and 7 January 1549. On that occasion the artist painted his portrait.

In a letter dated 6 December 1554, the King, who was then in London, notifies Vargas, his agent in Venice, that he has received Titian's *Venus and Adonis*. He adds that the canvas has been 'badly damaged by a fold in the very centre of it'. The defacing mark, in reality a slight one, can still be detected.

Philip's relations with Titian have been examined in detail by Beroqui. They account for the number and quality of the works acquired by the King from the artist over a period of nearly twenty-five years.

Yet this astonishing crop of masterpieces was not derived by Philip entirely from purchases. His collection was increased by two legacies, one from his father and the other from his aunt, Maria of Hungary, the Emperor's sister and wise counsellor, who died on 18 October 1558. She had assembled a number of masterpieces of painting and sculpture in her palaces at Mariemont and Bins. She did not care much for Philip, but she did leave him her pictures. They included some by Titian, such as *Sisyphus* and *Tityus,* the portraits of the Empress Isabella, Charles V on horseback and Philip II in armour and the figure of the Saviour from his *Noli me tangere,* which had been damaged. Rogier van der Weyden's *Deposition* also formed part of the bequest to Philip by Maria of Hungary. The works cited are all paintings of the very highest quality. Among the other items was also included the wonderful little panel of the Arnolfini couple, which Spain lost during the Dutch Wars of Independence. This picture is today one of those most highly prized in the National Gallery, London.

In order to appreciate the shrewdness of judgment in matters of art displayed by the Queen of Hungary and her nephew it is only necessary to read their observations on Titian's admirable portrait of Philip II in armour. It was through this painting, as is well known, that Mary Tudor, Queen of England, first made the acquaintance of her future husband. On 16 May 1551 the Prince, as he then was, sent the picture to his aunt, commenting 'The rapidity with which this portrait of myself in armour was executed is very evident. If I had more time, I would have it done again.' On 19 November 1553 Maria of Hungary forwarded the canvas to Simon Renard, who was to pass it on to the Queen of England. The Hungarian Queen wrote that the portrait was 'painted by Titian himself three years ago. Everyone considers it a very good likeness of the Prince at that time. Unfortunately the picture has suffered to some extent from the passage of time and also from its transport here from Augsburg. Nevertheless, the Queen will obtain a sufficient idea of what he looks like by studying the portrait in the correct light and at some little distance. For the said Titian's works are all of that kind. On a close view the sitter cannot be recognized.'

The above remarks could hardly have been made by ordinary amateurs of painting. The tone is that of genuine experts, capable of precise appreciation of Titian's luminous and free technique.

These quotations enable the artistic side of Philip's character to be better assessed. They also suggest why he approved the proposal of Felipe de Guevara, a courtier in attendance on Charles V. Guevara was the first person in Spain to express the hope that royal collections accumulated during the fifteenth and early sixteenth centuries would be exhibited, observing that 'while they are kept hidden away their value depreciates, for they are then deprived of the criticism of others and the views of their merits adopted by men of intelligence and imagination. This would not be the case if they were placed where great numbers of people could sometimes see them.'

As the ancient Alcazar of Madrid was undergoing repair, the royal collection could not be installed there. Accordingly, plans for the erection of another palace were put forward.

Ever since the fourteenth century the Castilian kings, all enthusiastic hunters, had been in the habit of frequenting a splendid forest near Madrid, with a circumference of over 60 miles, known as the Prado. In 1430 a castle had been built in the middle of it. In 1543 Charles V ordered this building to be pulled down and replaced by

SANCHEZ COELLO *Philip II*

*View of the Alcazar*

another, upon which work was immediately begun. The west door of this second structure bears the date 1547.

The Castilian Court had at that time no fixed place of residence. In 1565 Philip II decided that Madrid should be its centre. It was on that occasion that he thought of using the new Prado Palace as a picture gallery. A further idea was the construction at the gates of Madrid of a second Fontainebleau, probably as a compliment to his third wife, Isabelle de Valois, daughter of King Henry II of France, whom he had married in 1560.

An inventory of 1564 lists the paintings, ninety-six in all, which were afterwards placed in the new palace. The chief items were four portraits and three mythological works, the *Antiope* – erroneously named *Danaë* – by Titian, a *Hero and Leander* and *Arion as a Musician,* as well as various allegorical and *genre* pictures, some maps and only two paintings of religious subjects, a copy of van der Weyden's *Deposition* – today in the Escorial monastery – and the *Temptation of St Anthony* by Bosch.

It has sometimes been asserted that a palace situated some ten miles from the centre of Madrid could not have been very convenient for the visits of artists and others interested in painting, who would have preferred a gallery more easily accessible. But there is no point in such a criticism, for a document of 1582 proves that the intention was not to provide a museum unconditionally open to the public and that the Prado could only be visited by certain persons to whom formal invitations were extended. This first 'museum' or 'gallery' did not last long as such. On 13 March 1604 a fire destroyed a great part of the palace and a substantial number of the pictures it contained. It was soon rebuilt, but was only retained for its original purpose for fourteen years. In 1608 Juan Pantoja de la Cruz was engaged in reconstituting the series of royal portraits destined to adorn it.

But the project which fate had prevented from being realized at the Prado Palace was eventually carried out in the magnificent setting of the Escorial.

This building had been constructed at the orders of Philip II in fulfilment of a vow. In 1557, during the battle of St Quentin, the Spanish artillery had destroyed a church dedicated to St Lawrence. The King thereupon swore to erect a monastery in honour of the saint. The result was the Escorial, which was designed in the general form of a gridiron, in commemoration of the instrument of St Lawrence's martyrdom.

During the rest of his life the King despatched no less than eleven hundred and fifty paintings to the monastery. Such is the figure given by Fray Julian Zarco, who published in 1930 at Madrid an inventory of the jewels, pictures and other articles presented by Philip II (1571–1598). Obviously, not all these works were masterpieces; but the number thus authenticated is in itself imposing.

GRECO *The Dream of Philip II*

*View of the Escorial in the Seventeenth Century*

It is not certain whether the monastery could be regarded, during the century of its foundation, as a 'museum'. Undoubtedly, the works commissioned or acquired for its decoration were primarily, in the King's own view, indications of his personal piety. The modern mind may feel some surprise that certain pictures by Bosch or Patinir could be so considered. But it must be remembered that taste in these matters alters with the passage of time. Convincing proof of this point may be found in the admirable exposition by Fray José de Sigüenza of the value of the moral teaching illustrated by Bosch's triptych, *The Garden of Delights*. In referring to this strange artist's paintings the historian of the monastery states that they were situated

25

PANTOJA *Philip III*

in the cloisters, in the royal apartments, the chapter houses and the sacristy. He is careful to add that 'visitors could see them'.

The best works of the collection must have been assembled in the hall known as the *aula*. Among them were the *Annunciation* by Veronese and the *Nativity* by Tintoretto, both painted for the high altar. But as they could not be seen clearly in that position they had to be replaced by others. This *aula* came to be the nucleus of the rearrangement of the collection carried out by Velasquez, on the instructions of Philip IV, in the middle of the following century.

The number of pictures placed in the Escorial by Philip II has already been mentioned. But consultation of the inventories of those at the royal palaces of Madrid and the Prado, in addition to the Escorial archives, fills one with respect and gratitude towards the exceptional patron of art who gathered in so extraordinarily rich a harvest of paintings, an achievement for which he is so seldom given credit.

Beroqui has computed the grand total of pictures in the collection of Philip II. One hundred and seventeen works were at the Prado Palace and three hundred at the Madrid Alcazar, in addition to the eleven hundred and fifty at the Escorial, making one thousand five hundred and sixty-seven in all.


## Philip III

After the time of Philip II it becomes extremely difficult to calculate the numbers of these treasures. For in 1604 fifty portraits were burned in the fire at the Prado, and although Titian's famous *Jupiter and Antiope* escaped damage on that occasion this picture was later lost to Spain. It is today one of the finest works in the Louvre. The year of the Prado fire was also that in which items in the royal collections began to be transferred from one palace to another.

The character of Philip III was entirely different from that of his father. But by great good fortune his powerful favourite, the Duke of Lerma, was fond of painting. Lerma acquired Fra Angelico's

*Annunciation* and placed orders with Rubens, who came to Spain in 1603. This first visit of the artist resulted in the production of a dozen panels, still retained in the collection, for the duke. They include Rubens's *Apostles, Democritus, Heraclitus* and *Archimedes.*

## Philip IV

First-hand evidence exists that in the seventeenth century visitors came to the Escorial for the express purpose of studying its collection of works of art. It is no less interesting to recall that Pacheco, the painter and theorist who was the father-in-law of Velasquez, twice refers, in his *Art of Painting,* to his visit to the Escorial in 1611. He also mentions visits paid to the monastery by Velasquez and Rubens.

The painter Vincencio Carducho reports in his 'Eighth Dialogue' that in 1633 he was shown *'during his Majesty's absence,* all the pictures at the Alcazar of Madrid'. Some forty years later another painter, Jusepe Martinez, relates in the following terms a conversation between Velasquez and Philip IV which probably took place in 1648. 'His Majesty intimated to him his desire to found a gallery decorated with paintings and requested him to seek out artists of renown and select their best works. Velasquez replied: "Your Majesty should not be satisfied with pictures available to anyone." The King asked: "How can that be arranged?" Velasquez answered: "I will undertake, Sire, subject to Your Majesty's approval, to go to Rome and Venice, find the best works by Titian, Veronese, Bassano, Raphael, Parmigianino and other artists of that calibre and buy them."'

As is well known, Velasquez visited Italy accordingly. On his return in 1651 he brought with him pictures, statues and moulds for casting in bronze.

The King's plans for a gallery at Madrid went no further for the time being. But the results of the visit of Velasquez to Italy were immediately evident at the Escorial. Contemporary documents attest the fact.

VELASQUEZ *Self-portrait*

In a letter partially damaged by fire but written prior to 17 December 1654 Don Luis Méndez de Haro, Marques del Carpio, requests Don Alonso de Cardenas to buy pictures for Philip IV in London. He states: 'As the Escorial is constantly visited, throughout the year, by great numbers of foreigners who come to admire and wonder at it, I should be glad if inferior works in the collection could be removed and replaced by better ones.' This phrase is clearly expressive of a typical museum curator's outlook.

Some years later Fray Francisco de los Santos, the contemporary historian of the Escorial, refers, in his *Description* of the monastery, published in 1657, to the *capitulos* or chapter houses. He writes: 'The King, in his magnanimity and piety, has decided to decorate them, like the sacristy, with various paintings of greater merit, which are being searched for in accordance with his instructions.' The sacristy was then considered the most suitable place in which to exhibit the best pictures. It could be visited by anyone who requested permission to do so. As the chapter houses were very little used by the monks, the King had decided to adorn them in the same fashion as the sacristy. Fray Francisco's text was undoubtedly composed more than a year before publication. In point of fact, according to Palomino, Philip had ordered Velasquez, as early as 1656, to despatch to the Escorial 'forty-one original paintings, for which the artist in question drew up descriptive memoranda, noting their qualities, history, executants and present locations'.

The idea was therefore taking shape of a royal picture gallery in the true sense of the term. The character of the future Prado can already be discerned in the then unrivalled collection of Philip IV. It was also then that some of the present basic items were assembled. For in the nineteenth century the Escorial sent more than a hundred and forty paintings to the Prado.

Philip had succeeded in forming his exceptional collection by adding to all the pictures he had inherited those bought at the auction in London, when the collection of Charles I, after that monarch's execution, was dispersed, as well as the works acquired in Italy through the efforts of his viceroys and Velasquez. Further additions

VELASQUEZ *Philip IV*

included canvases painted by Rubens during his second visit to
Spain in 1628–1629 and the very numerous orders subsequently
placed with him by the King. Pictures were also sent from Flanders
by the Infanta Archduchess Isabella Clara Eugenia. Finally, this
already dazzling assemblage of masterpieces was still further enlarged

by the productions of Velasquez during the twenty-seven years when he worked almost exclusively for Philip, his personal friend.

The royal patron of art, moreover, was most anxious to obtain paintings by artists not yet or only unsatisfactorily represented in his collections, such as Raphael. Unfortunately the King's ardour in this connection led him to perpetrate or to countenance, on two occasions, illegal acquisitions. As these cases were exceptional, there being no question here of the 'spoils of war' or compulsory deliveries, it may be of interest to report the facts relevant to the only works in the Prado which came into Philip's possession as the result of a certain degree of coercion.

The first of these, Raphael's *Way to Calvary*, had been painted for the chapel of the Olivetan house of Santa Maria dello Spasimo at Palermo. Hence it is most commonly known as '*Lo Spasimo di Sicilia*'. The Count of Ayala, viceroy of the Province, attempted to buy the picture for Philip IV. But the local authorities were reluctant to sell it. The viceroy eventually forced them to do so, though the price agreed was very high, amounting to the payment of an annuity of 4000 ducats to the monastery and a lump sum of 500 ducats for the prior who took the painting to Madrid.

In the second case the Duke of Medina de las Torres, viceroy of Naples, did his utmost to obtain Raphael's *Madonna of the Fish* from the Superior General of the Dominican Order in Naples. Neither the prior of the monastery nor the lay authorities would listen to him. But the Duke, after long negotiations, at last achieved his object. By the end of his term as viceroy he was able to present the picture to the King.

Philip, like a true connoisseur, kept himself informed of the sales of works of art which took place all over Europe. His vigilance in this respect enabled him to procure items of very great value.

As already mentioned, he bought paintings at the auction of the collection of Charles I of England. In this affair he employed Alonso de Cardenas, with whom he corresponded through his minister and favourite Luis Méndez de Haro. Unfortunately two fires at the palace of Liria in the nineteenth century destroyed some of these

VAN DYCK *King Charles I*

letters, so that the list of masterpieces thus acquired by Philip, which can be identified by the monogram C. R. (Carolus Rex) below a crown on the back of the canvas, remains incomplete. But they include Mantegna's *Death of the Virgin*, Raphael's *Holy Family ('Perla')*, Titian's *General del Vasto addressing his Troops*, *Charles V with a Dog* and *Venus with the Organ-player*, Andrea del Sarto's *Virgin and Child with Saint and Angel*, Veronese's *Marriage at Cana* and *Christ and the Centurion*, Tintoretto's *Christ washing the Feet of*

33

*his Disciples,* Palma Giovane's *David and Goliath* and *Conversion of St Paul* and a self-portrait by Dürer. Correggio's *Noli me tangere* came indirectly from the same sale. It was generously presented to Philip by the Duke of Medina de las Torres.

On the death of Rubens a similar sale was held of his collection, housed in the artist's sumptuous mansion at Antwerp. On that occasion Philip was able to purchase a self-portrait by Titian, van Dyck's *Betrayal* and *Crowning with Thorns* and some splendid pictures by Rubens himself, including *The Three Graces, The Garden of Love* and *Peasants Dancing,* together with the portraits of Marie de'Medici and the Cardinal Infante on horseback, the *St George and the Dragon,* the *Supper at Emmaus* and *Nymphs and Satyrs.* It was at this time that the Cardinal Infante, the King's brother and Governor of Flanders, saved Rubens's 'nudes' from the flames. Helena Fourment, widow of the painter, who had often been his model, wished, in a fit of excessive modesty, to destroy them. The Infante, through a Jesuit who acted as the confessor of this over-scrupulous lady, persuaded her to revoke a decision which would have been disastrous from an artistic standpoint.

King Philip acquired fresh paintings at the auction of the collection of the Marques de Leganes. These included Jan 'Velvet' Brueghel's *Vision of St Hubert,* Titian's *Salome* and *Federigo II Gonzaga* and Tintoretto's *Portrait of a Jesuit.*

To all these acquisitions must be added the gifts received by the King. His tastes were so well known that pictures were often offered to him. Queen Christina of Sweden, for example, sent him Dürer's *Adam* and *Eve.* The Marques de Leganes gave him Quellyn's *Immaculate Conception,* and the portrait supposed to be that of Sebastian Veniero by Tintoretto. The Duke of Medina de las Torres presented him with Jan Brueghel's *Touch* and the *Deer Hunt* by Paul de Vos, while from the Admiral of Castile he obtained the *Martyrdom of St Mennas* by Veronese.

Yet this long list of works in the collection of Philip IV is still not complete. It should comprise also those ordered by the King from the great artists of his time, such as five landscapes painted for him

JUAN BAUPTISTA DE MADRAZO *The Pardo*

by Claude le Lorrain, twelve large canvases executed in Rome and mentioned by Sandrart. Gentileschi's *Finding of Moses* and many more.

Philip's initiative was also responsible for some important groups of works of the same type, such as the equestrian portraits by Velasquez decorating the 'Apartment of the Kingdom' in the Buen Retiro Palace, the pictures celebrating victories gained at the beginning of the reign, like the *Surrender of Breda* of Velasquez and Zurbarán's *Labours of Hercules* and those adorning the Torre de la Parada, a hunting lodge in the Prado woods, for which Velasquez painted his hunting portraits and *Aesop* and *Menippus*. It was for this building, also, that the fertile imagination of Rubens created, with a magical facility and beauty of style, an exuberant series of productions inspired by the Metamorphoses of Ovid. Some of these grandiose compositions were executed and signed by his pupils. But it may be conjectured that those unsigned came from the master's own hand.

The works placed in the Torre de la Parada were removed immediately after the King's death. The Buen Retiro Palace kept its treasures rather longer. Some idea of the importance of the Buen Retiro collection may be formed from the fact that a century later the painter Napoli believed that Philip IV had intended to turn the palace into a picture gallery.

In any case it is certain that the royal collections were used in exactly the same way as those of a real museum. The most convincing proof of this fact is that Spanish painting of the Golden Age and in particular the School of Madrid would not be historically intelligible if the artists concerned had not been able to study the Flemish and Italian pictures assembled in the royal palaces. Mazo, Carreño, Cerezo, Claudio Coello and even Murillo could not have developed as they did without knowledge of the works of Titian, Veronese, Rubens and van Dyck thus preserved by Philip.

On 14 September 1665 the King, who was to die three days later, made a will in which he gave instructions for 'all the pictures to become Crown property ... they are to remain in position after my death in the Royal Palace of Madrid and not one of them is to pass out of its keeping.' This testamentary disposition created the juridical institution of what used to be called the 'Royal Patrimony', the legal basis upon which the Prado collection was established. The arrangement was respected by all the kings of Spain. But the honour of its inauguration is due only to Philip IV.

*Charles II*

No such resolute spirit was manifested by his successor, Charles II. A sick man, he oscillated between influences of the most diverse

36

character. Yet the weakness of his mind did not prevent him from appreciating, like his ancestors, the art of painting. He bought pictures, as they had. At the auction which followed the death of the Marques de Eliche in 1687 he acquired the *Holy Family with St Anne* by Rubens, Crespi's *Pietà*, the *Infant Christ with St John* by Jordaens and the remarkable designs painted by Rubens for the tapestry representing the *Triumph of the Church*, which had been commissioned by the Infanta Archduchess Isabella Clara Eugenia for the nunnery of the Royal Barefoot Sisterhood in Madrid.

From a political point of view the reign of Charles II may be regarded as a period of complete decadence, the King himself suffering in person all the misfortunes which all his weaknesses brought upon him. Yet it must be repeated that his attitude to the arts has left him with a certain amount of prestige.

The collection he bequeathed was to a considerable extent inherited by him, though he had added a few items. It was imposing both in quantity and quality. The inventories list five thousand five hundred and thirty-nine pictures. Of these one thousand six hundred and twenty-two were at the Escorial. They had been assembled under royal patronage but did not form part of the Patrimony. These statistics cannot be considered dry when it is remembered that a large number of the works in question are masterpieces.

Another attractive aspect of the personality of Charles II, the 'Bewitched', as he was called, is the very clear notion he had of his duty. He would not allow the slightest diminution of his artistic inheritance. His second wife, Queen Mariana of Neuburg, wished to give her father the enormous *Adoration of the Kings* by Rubens, now at the Prado. A shrewd woman, she thought it would be easy to obtain this favour from her husband, for the picture did not adorn the royal apartments but had been relegated to a room which was only occupied in the summer. She brought great pressure to bear on Charles. But his retort was unexpectedly firm and ingenious. 'The picture is not hung in that room,' he said. 'It constitutes part of the decorations and is consequently included in the Patrimony of the Crown.' This reply became so well known that when His

596 <sub>1077</sub>

RANC *Philip V*

Highness the Elector, Mariana's father, coveted another work, *Christ disputing with the Doctors,* by Veronese, his agent dared not openly proclaim his master's presumptuous demand. The emissary's task was all the more delicate because it had been intended, in reliance upon the supposed imbecility of the monarch, to replace the Veronese by a work of Luca Giordano. Such anecdotes effectively illustrate the interest taken by the princes of the House of Austria in painting, even when their personalities were otherwise undistinguished. It is remarkable that so feeble a king as Charles II showed himself quite capable of making good the omissions in the will of his father, Philip IV, and of actually adding to the number of works of art permanently included in the Patrimony of the Crown.

## Philip V

The eighteenth century brought about no change in the attitude of the kings to painting. Charles II died in 1700 and the new century began with a new dynasty. A Bourbon prince ascended the throne of Spain as Philip V. He was a great-grandson, through his grandmother Maria Theresa, of Philip IV. Though educated at the Court of Louis XIV and intending, when he crossed the Pyrenees, to make the Court of Spain French, the new king continued the artistic policy followed by the Austrian dynasty for the past two hundred years. In this activity he was supported by his wife Isabella Farnese, who had been born in Parma and brought up in Italy.

Philip and the Queen each had a collection of their own. The St Andrew's Cross of Burgundy, indicating works belonging to the King, and the fleur-de-lis stamped on those owned by Isabella, are to be found on dozens of canvases in the Prado. Philip possessed three hundred and eighteen and his wife nine hundred and eighty-nine. Both collections were added to the royal Patrimony. Some, in fact, already formed part of it.

The palaces were thus enriched by many of the paintings of Teniers, Snyders, Fyt, Valkenborch and other Flemings who produced

HOUASSE *View of the Escorial*

genre studies, landscapes and hunting scenes. The collections of Philip and Isabella also contained some of the few Dutch pictures to be seen at the Prado, as well as its two paintings by Watteau and, rather more surprising, early works by Murillo, acquired after the visit of the royal family to Seville in 1729/30. In this way the artistic policy of the new dynasty, shrewdly directed and steadily pursued, resulted in a collection of paintings not only prodigious in quantity and quality but also highly original in the choice it made among the various schools represented.

In 1734 fire broke out in the quarters adjoining the Alcazar of Madrid, occupied by the French artist Jean Ranc. He had been celebrating Christmas Eve there. The flames spread to such an extent that the palace was destroyed. Five hundred and thirty-seven pictures – the number was most carefully calculated – perished. Many others were damaged.

The works acquired by Philip V and Queen Isabella may be regarded as a kind of compensation for the devastating losses then suffered by the royal collections. Those of Philip and Isabella had been formed before the catastrophe and served to fill a good many gaps. The King and Queen, for instance, had bought twenty-seven paintings by Murillo, of whose work they formerly possessed few examples. Sixteen of those then purchased are still in the Prado.

The reconstruction of the palace proved extremely burdensome. But the Spanish sovereigns were so fond of pictures that this costly undertaking hardly restricted the number of purchases made by Ferdinand VI and Charles III. The ceiling decorations were entrusted by them to Corrado Ciaquinto, Giovanni Battista Tiepolo, and Anton Raphael Mengs.

*Charles III*

This King bought four collections, those of the Marques de la Enseñada, the Marques de Los Llanos, the Duquesa del Arco, and Don Juan Kelly. The first, which Charles acquired in 1768, was a notable body of work, including such masterpieces as the equestrian portrait of Olivares by Velasquez, Rembrandt's *Artemisia*, Tintoretto's *Judith and Holofernes, Christ with an Angel* by Alonso Cano and seven pictures by Murillo.

The idea of founding a museum was several times revived by Spanish artists and lovers of painting. Anton Raphael Mengs writes, in the course of a most interesting letter of 1775 to the traveller Ponz: 'I wish that all the valuable pictures at present dispersed among the other royal residences could be collected in the Palace' – i. e. the new royal palace at Madrid – 'and placed in a *gallery* worthy of so eminent a monarch. I could then compose, to the best of my ability, a treatise for the guidance of those interested, dealing with every artist, from the oldest . . . to the most recent. As it is, since the Court has never considered the establishment of such a collection, my discussion of the painters of various epochs will necessarily be incomplete.'

The German painter here argues in favour of the advantages of a national gallery and seems to advocate systematic arrangement of it, a surprising innovation at this period. But he makes no reference

MENGS *Charles III*

to the precedents mentioned above, dating back a hundred and twenty-five years. He evidently supposes himself to be the first person in Spain to have thought of such a thing, an indication of the complacency of a foreign artist, immensely proud of having visited capitals other than his own.

In 1774 reconstruction of the palace of Goyeneche in the Alcala Avenue at Madrid was completed. A Latin inscription on the building proclaimed: 'King Charles III has here united nature and art under one roof for the benefit of the public. 1774.' Actually, this edifice was intended for the St Ferdinand Royal Academy of Fine Art, founded in 1752, and at the same time for the Museum of Natural History. In order to adorn the interior and facilitate teaching in the Academy the King decreed, in 1774, the transfer to this establishment of the pictures formerly in the possession of the suppressed communities of the Company of Jesus. In so doing he created the second nucleus of works for the future Museum.

But other paintings of inestimable value still remained sequestered. The royal palaces contained a wonderful series of depictions of the nude either commissioned or purchased by the 'austere' Philip II or by Philip IV. These pictures had not corrupted the piety of the first-named of these sovereigns, nor of his son Philip III who was named the 'Devout'. Moreover the paintings by Rubens had, as mentioned above, been preserved by the intervention of the Cardinal-Infante. Yet Charles III, though he had ordered the excavation of Herculaneum, as well as protecting the friends of Voltaire and expelling the Jesuits, considered these nudes scandalous. It may have been under the influence of his confessor, Fray Joaquin de Eleta, of Alcantara, an irreconcilable fanatic, that the King apparently decided to have the masterpieces by Titian, Rubens, and Dürer burned. Mengs protested: Charles agreed not to order this fearful holocaust, but he advised his son Charles IV to have it carried out. The Marques de Santa Cruz, Lord High Chamberlain and official adviser to the Royal Academy of Fine Art, eventually saved these precious paintings from the flames, but only on condition that they were locked up in a room at the Academy, where they were placed in 1792 and 1796, remaining there for several years, until 1827. It is impossible to say how far the prohibition of study of these admirable works was respected. One may assume that members of the Academy and artists of mature age were allowed access to this astonishing hidden treasure. For it was laid down that prior authorization was required to view the pictures. They were exhibited elsewhere during the occupation of Madrid by the Napoleonic troops. But on that occasion, unfortunately, two canvases by Titian, his *Sleeping Venus* and a *Danaë,* disappeared.

The devotion of the Spanish kings to painting is again evident at the beginning of the reign of Charles IV. He was very far from a brilliant sovereign intellectually. His principal amusements were the chase, his violin and his carpentry workshop. Yet he revealed considerable energy as a collector, assembling a number of works in his delightful 'Prince's House' at the Escorial. Julian Zarco has published the inventory of them, listing four hundred and twenty-one items. Not all of these, however, were pictures. Moreover, some of the paintings were borrowed from other palaces and consequently already belonged to the Crown.

The future Charles IV, while still Prince of Asturias, bought Raphael's *Portrait of a Cardinal,* the two panels by the Master of Flémalle, *Abraham's Sacrifice* by Andrea del Sarto, Ribera's *Apostles* and a number of other works of equal standing. In this case too the masterpieces acquired by the King lend his personality more substance in our eyes. Charles IV certainly deserves his place among those who contributed most to the enrichment of the Prado collection.

He was obliged to cease such activities on his abdication; nevertheless, two last steps which he took in this field remain to be recorded. In 1804, while on a visit to Valencia, the King bought some important pictures by Juan de Juanes, which are also now in the Prado. His interest in painting, moreover, continued to be so intense that even after he had lost his throne and grown old he resumed collecting in Rome.

Study of the origins of the Prado Museum cannot ignore the influence exercised on Spanish plans by events in France during the revolutionary period. The motion to establish a museum at the Louvre was made by Bertrand Barère before the Constituent Assembly on 26 March 1791, and passed by the Assembly on 28 March. The proposal was soon echoed in Madrid. On 1 September 1800, the minister Urquijo repeated an order he had already issued for the transfer of several works by Murillo from Seville to Madrid, stating

GOYA *Charles IV*

that these 'measures are in agreement with those supported by all the civilized nations of Europe, where steps are being taken to establish schools and museums in the capital cities'.

On 28 June 1803, Godoy revoked Urquijo's decree but confirmed the principle which had inspired it, for he refers to 'His Majesty's Museum'. In a further order issued on 8 July the Museum to be established in the capital is again mentioned.

Don Pedro Beroqui, that tireless researcher into the history of the Prado, has discovered a document proving that during those years the foundation of a Museum at Madrid was discussed. It takes the form of a letter in which the author Vargas Ponce writes to Cean Bermudez: 'Some of the best canvases of Murillo would be appropriately hung in a *gallery* containing the pick of our paintings. In my opinion the wing which is still to be added to the new palace should be erected with this end in view.'

He is here alluding to the proposed construction of a building to balance that set up on the Plaza de la Armeria in the reign of Charles III.

Many ideas, plans, experiments and partially realized projects for a great museum in the Spanish capital – regarded as including the Escorial – were under consideration between 1563 and 1808, the year in which the eighteenth century, for Spaniards, really ended. The birth of the Prado, accordingly, was preceded by a very long and laborious gestation.

ABORTIVE PROJECTS BY JOSEPH BONAPARTE

AND FERDINAND VII

Such was the name given to the Museum which the usurping king, Joseph Bonaparte, desired to establish. The project was never realized. For it was frustrated, like so many other of his plans, by the calamities of the time and above all by the obstacle he described to his brother, the Emperor – a 'nation of twelve million souls, exasperated beyond endurance'.

Joseph had a discerning mind. He had never been under any illusions about his reign, which he knew could not last. On 19 November 1810, he wrote to his uncle, Cardinal Fesch: 'I know this country better than anyone and am well aware of what I can and cannot promise if I am to be a success.' He admitted even at this date that he longed to return to Naples or else to retire to an 'estate a hundred leagues from Paris'. He had clearly foreseen the future from the start. 'No, Sire,' he told his brother, 'you are wrong. Your career of glory will be checked in Spain.' Nevertheless, Joseph did his best to govern the nation assigned to him in the distribution of the countries of Europe among the Bonaparte family.

A decree of 20 August 1809, prescribed the suppression of the religious orders and the sequestration of their property, including paintings. The works in question were collected in two of the vacant monasteries, and will be referred to later. On 20 December of the same year Urquijo, who had issued the order of 1800 already mentioned, countersigned a further decree outlining two forthcoming measures. Everyone was at liberty to form his own opinion of these proposals. But the second disgusted Spaniards. Article I read: 'A museum for pictures, containing selected examples of the different schools, will be established in Madrid. For this purpose the paintings required to complete the collection thus decreed will be removed from all public institutions, including the palaces.' Article II stated: 'A comprehensive collection of works by famous artists of the Spanish School will be formed, with a view to presenting it to our august brother, Emperor of the French. We shall express to him at the same time our desire to see the collection placed in one of

FLAUGIER *Joseph Bonaparte*

the halls of the Napoleon Museum, where it will constitute a monument to the glory of Spanish artists and a guarantee of the sincerest possible union between the two nations.'

The other Articles of the decree have no bearing on the subject of the Prado. Article II, in accordance with which fifty pictures were selected and sent to Paris, is only mentioned for the sake of its vivid illustration of the contemporary atmosphere.

On 22 August of the following year Joseph ordered the proposed museum to be established in the Buenavista palace, a building which had been commenced by the Duchess of Alba. This much misunderstood lady is famous as having inspired drawings, engravings and paintings by Goya. But she was not, as has been asserted, the object of his lifelong passion. The Duchess, however, was unable to complete the building. It was bought by the citizens of Madrid and presented to the Court favourite and all-powerful minister of the day, Manuel Godoy. He extended the structure, which he decorated and furnished. But he could make no further use of the property, for the riots of 19 March 1808, brought about his fall from power.

Both Urquijo, who now took up plans he had formulated eight years before, and Frédéric Quilliet, a Frenchman whom the Spaniards rather disliked but whom Joseph had appointed Curator of Works of Art in the royal palaces, were concerned in carrying out the King's decree.

They did very little. But it is probable that pictures formerly in the possession of the suppressed monasteries were added, under the roof of the palace intended to house the proposed splendours of 'King Joseph's Museum', to the collection formed by Godoy. At any rate the paintings from the monasteries were found in the palace on the return of Ferdinand VII.

Joseph Bonaparte's prophecies of 1810 were followed, until 1813, by years of tragedy which only confirmed his judgment. The period was hardly propitious to the establishment of a museum. But the plans and preparations made may have given Joseph a taste for painting. For both during his preliminary retirement in Switzerland and subsequently in the United States he collected pictures.

Spain has far from agreeable recollections of Joseph Bonaparte. But it would be unjust not to recognize his high-mindedness and his clear realization that the prodigious adventure of the Empire was doomed to fail.

On 10 April 1835, his melancholy experiences impelled him to write, in noble terms, to his uncle the Cardinal. 'All the former supporters of the Emperor', he observes, 'have made a separate peace with their enemies. Yet their property is confiscated and plundered, while to him a statue is to be erected. We are slandered. He is lauded to the skies. No one treated our mother and ourselves more generously, after Napoleon's death, than Pius VII. It was because he knew himself to be the Vicar of Christ and his soul in Christ's keeping that the Pope celebrated Mass that day for the repose of his ancient enemy and consoled our mother.'

A man capable of such lofty sentiments was far from deserving the travesties of his character current among Spaniards, who thus meanly avenged the wounds inflicted upon them by the armies of his brother.

## The Museum of Ferdinand VII

As soon as he returned to Spain Ferdinand ordered the Academy to retrieve the pictures which had been dispersed in various buildings by the foreign Government and bring them together in one place to form a museum. On 15 June 1814, the Academy met to discuss the question of which accommodation to select for the purpose, the so-called Custom House adjoining their own premises, which later became the Finance Ministry, or the Buenavista Palace. Some of the members had also thought of the house in which the royal collection of crystal was kept, situated in the street today known as that of the Marques de Culas but which was then called Turk Street.

A majority preferred the Buenavista Palace. But they were very well aware what heavy expenses would be required to make good its dilapidated condition.

On the following 5 July the King, accompanied by his brother Don Carlos Maria Isidro and his uncle Don Antonio, visited the Academy. At the reception ceremony a royal decree, dated the previous day, was read out, assigning the Buenavista Palace to the Academy. The members were to move into the building and establish in it 'a gallery of pictures, engravings, statues, architectural

GOYA *Ferdinand VII in the Uniform of a General*

plans and other objects of artistic value, conveniently and effectively exhibited, both to provide instruction ... and to satisfy the honourable curiosity of Spaniards and foreigners, as well as bestowing upon Spain a glory she so richly deserves.'

The move was to be made at once. But fresh obstacles from various sources arose. On the one hand, the reconstituted monasteries claimed the restoration of their sequestered pictures. On the other hand, the reconstruction and transformation of the palace would need the expenditure of enormous sums which the Academy could not raise. Those at its disposal had been spent after no more than five weeks of work. But the decisive check to the project was administered by the Royal Council of Castile, which advanced weighty legal objections to the plan. Since the palace formed part of the property sequestered by Godoy, it was not included among the buildings confiscated by the State and consequently could not be disposed of by the latter.

On 21 August the Academy relinquished the Buenavista Palace. Ferdinand, in confirming their decision, promised to 'provide a location worthy of his lofty aims and desires and not subject to the same drawbacks as the Buenavista Palace'.

Thus the Museum of King Ferdinand, like that of King Joseph, perished before it was born.

THE CREATION OF THE PRADO

One after the other the efforts of Joseph Bonaparte and Ferdinand VII to establish a picture gallery in the Buenavista Palace had failed. But, in a wholly unexpected way, the existence of a large building dominated by the monastery of St Jerome, in the Prado Avenue, which had been for a century the most crowded resort in the capital, was to introduce a determining factor into solving the problem.

As already mentioned, Charles III, in 1774, had brought under a single roof, in the Goyeneche mansion situated in the Alcala Avenue, the Natural History collection and that of the St Ferdinand Royal Academy of Fine Art. It is probable that his minister, the Count of Floridablanca, considered such a conjunction somewhat unsuitable or at any rate judged the accommodation to be too restricted for the convenient maintenance of two such dissimilar bodies. At all events he suggested to the King that an Academy of Science might be established, since an Academy of Literature and History and an Academy of Fine Art, founded respectively by Philip V and Ferdinand VI, already existed. Charles gave orders for plans to be drawn up to this end. They had been completed in 1780, though since shelved. The minister had seemed less interested in science than in the erection of an imposing edifice provided with a long covered colonnade for pedestrians. He was of the opinion that such a frontage would increase the dignified aspect of the Prado Avenue.

The King finally directed, in 1785, that a building should be constructed to serve as a Museum of Natural Science near the recently established Botanical Gardens.

The project was entrusted to the architect Juan de Villanueva (1739–1811) who submitted his first plans on 30 May 1785. Little information is available as to the progress of the works. In 1787 important modifications of the original designs were introduced: the idea of a covered colonnade for the frontage was dropped. On 10 October 1788, Floridablanca resigned his office as minister. In a valedictory speech he referred to 'the magnificent Palace of Science ... already rising before our eyes', in which he assured his hearers that 'majesty, solidity and utility rival elegance and beauty', adding that 'the works are already far advanced . . . and the remarkably comprehensive Natural History Collection, Laboratory and Science Academy will find therein a lodging worthy of their merits'.

A piece of evidence hitherto neglected proves that the edifice, including walls, vaulting and roof, was probably completed in 1806 and certainly before 1808.

In 1806 Don Nicolas de la Cruz y Bahamonde, Count of Maule, a cultured gentleman born in Cadiz, who enjoyed collecting works of art and had lived in America, began publication of a work entitled *Travels through Spain, France and Italy*. The format and typography of the book resemble those of earlier productions by Don Antonio Ponz, *Travels through Spain* (1776) and *Travels beyond Spain* (1785). Volume 10 of the Count's work deals with Madrid. Much of the text discusses Spanish history, but monuments and art collections in the capital are also mentioned. The author, in this unjustly neglected production, uses notes and recollections dating from before the War of Independence: certain pages bearing the date 1806 are proof positive that he was in Madrid that year. His references to the construction of the Natural Science building are the most important documentary evidence we possess on the subject. They afford a precise notion of the progress of the works.

He writes: 'Of all the public edifices the magnificent Museum is the most worthy of our concentrated attention . . . the main frontage comprises a peristyle of six massive Doric columns below and a gallery above composed of twenty-eight Ionic columns, fourteen on each side, combined with twenty-eight pilasters. The jutting angles are quite pleasing. On the side facing the Botanical Gardens a fine porch is to be seen, adorned with four fluted Corinthian columns, unfinished. On the opposite or east [he should have written *north*] side there is a second, smaller porch, with two Ionic columns . . . A further magnificent structure, oval in form and not yet finished, is to project south [he should have written *east*] from the central hall . . . Within the building other fine halls, some long, others circular, will be found . . . together with an extensive basement. The upper part of the

GOYA *Juan de Villanueva*

*The Prado*

Museum resembles a sort of attic . . . It would be advantageous if the architect, Don Juan Villanueva, in charge of the works, were to publish his plans as soon as the building is completed and compose a detailed account of a structure of such great merit. The frontage at present lacks light, but will not do so after the site has been cleared and the adjacent walls on the Prado Avenue demolished. The edifice will then make a very fine impression.'

From this passage it may be deduced that of the three most conspicuous façades only that on the south still lacked, at the time, a few of its Corinthian columns. A porch was then being erected on the east front, but it was never finished. The oval building was not completed before the middle of the nineteenth century.

Other statements by the Count contradict an assertion often repeated. In fact, the ground floor only had been walled in and vaulted when the troops of Napoleon used the building to stable their horses.

The poet Juan Nicasio Gallego was not merely being carried away by lyrical enthusiasm when he composed an ode read to the Royal Academy of Fine Art on 24 September 1808, while the French troops were absent from Madrid. He wrote:

*The Prado: the front with the statue of Velasquez*

Now in my dreams
I see the future and behold
all the immensity of this most glorious Museum . . .
and in those royal halls
once given over to such usage vile
art sparkling with even brighter lustre
than ever art did shine
in Greece, in Rome, in Tyre or Sidon.

The fifth line is soon explained. The poet was not exaggerating. For at that period not only the section of the building which mainly faced west but also the north entrance to what is now the second floor of the Museum were turned into stables.

This 'usage vile', together with the general vicissitudes of the war and sheer neglect, were factors contributing to the serious deterioration of the structure during these tragic years. Tiles and lead were stripped from the roof, so that damage was done to the walls and vaulting. These circumstances are described by the architect López Aguado in the *Semanario Pintoresco Ilustrado*, page 183.

Those who may be interested in the Museum as a majestic and beautiful piece of architecture will find its character analysed in detail by F. Chueca Goitia and C. de Miguel in their *Life and Works of the Architect Juan de Villanueva* published in Madrid in 1949, and also in the substantial study by the first-named of these authors entitled *The Prado Museum* in the 'Architectural Guides Series' (Madrid, 1952).

Chueca ingeniously discerns in the ground plan of the edifice three monumental units the sum of which constitutes a highly original design. These are the forecourt, comprising the Ionic porch and rotunda of the west front, erected at ground level; a kind of basilica with a Doric porch on the east front, with the apse covering the area of the great hall of Velasquez, which was originally intended to occupy the entire space now divided into two floors; and finally a palace with an extensive vestibule and interior court, comprising the main structure to the south.

The modifications and enlargements carried out at the Museum during the last hundred years have rendered it difficult today to distinguish the various units referred to.

Chueca's interpretations of the architecture calls attention to Villanueva's skill and knowledge. But the analysis is not exhaustive: it hardly accounts for the low rotunda, which was formerly half underground and could only be artificially lit. The view that its purpose was functional does not solve the problem raised by the quality of its materials, by its frieze and by the niches which were undoubtedly intended for practical use.

Reliable documents are lacking on which to base understanding of the separate objects for which each of the halls in this great building was designed. Such evidence alone could prevent erroneous views being formed of the purposes of some of them, for example the basement situated west and south, now used for exhibitions and lectures. The entrance is so fine and the architectural design of the hall so grand that it is impossible to suppose that it was meant to be a lumber-room. Yet, on the other hand, so little daylight enters the place that it could hardly have been intended to serve any other object. The apartment known today as the 'low rotunda', its gallery and the Spanish Altarpieces Room, in addition to the basement just mentioned, are so arranged as to suggest, not very plausibly, that Villanueva may have had artificial lighting in mind.

If it had not been for the war, the building might well have come into use as a Museum of Natural History during the year 1808. The damage it suffered as a result of the fighting is indicated clearly enough by the Comte de la Forest, Napoleon's ambassador at Madrid. On 20 September 1811, a month after the architect's death, he reported to the Duke of Bassano a meeting of the State Council.

'By an oversight the reading of a further proposed decree was called for, dealing with the question of completing the Prado Museum. But the smiles with which all the members greeted the reading caused it to be broken off.' Everyone in Madrid knew that owing to lack of funds there could be no hope of finishing the building.

Incongruities are inevitable in all structures not completed by the architect responsible for the plans. Modifications were necessarily introduced into an edifice conceived for a purpose very different from that subsequently envisaged. Moreover, the development of the institution which had been lodged in the building for a hundred and thirty-seven years had led to some extension of the accommodation. Despite all such effects, however, the Prado Museum remains one of the finest monuments in Madrid and possibly the most important example of Spanish neo-classical architecture. Adaptation to the needs of a picture gallery has actually improved it, especially since the introduction of artificial lighting. Villanueva's structure has proved in every respect responsive to the use now made of it. Its proportions, its resistance to drastic changes of temperature, its relative humidity, helping to preserve the paintings, as well as the absence of ancient decorative features which would have had to be left undisturbed, and finally its situation, to which the plans were originally subordinate and which allowed its enlargement without disfigurement of the frontage on the Prado Avenue, were all advantageous to the function of a picture gallery. The ancient part of the building, however, could in my opinion still be improved and better adapted to serve the general purpose.

*The Founders, Ferdinand VII and Isabella de Braganza*

Two hundred and fifty years had not been long enough for the ideas, desires and plans promoted in this connection to be carried into effect. Yet, when Ferdinand VII returned to his throne, in the midst of difficulties of every kind, no more than five years, thanks to the rapidity with which Spain has always recovered after critical periods, sufficed for the formation of the nucleus of a truly great Museum.

As already emphasized, the existence of the magnificent Prado building proved decisive for the achievement of this result.

Reference has been made above to the intervention of the Council of Castile, which caused the abandonment of Ferdinand's project for

VICENTE LOPEZ *Isabella de Braganza*

a museum to be organized by the Academy in the Buenavista Palace at its own expense and from funds arising in consequence of the suppression of the monasteries and other similar measures. The relevant papers include an expression of opinion, dated 29 November 1814, by the three representatives of the Council. They write: 'It would be preferable, as the question relates to a Museum, to make use of the famous building erected *for that purpose* by the august grandfather and father of Your Majesty in the Prado Avenue, at a cost of several millions, rather than allow it to become a complete ruin while more central or more convenient accommodation is being found.'

Accordingly, on 26 December, Ferdinand issued a royal decree beginning with the words: 'I agree with the Council's opinion . . .' This simple measure enabled positive steps to be taken for the establishment of the Museum.

Some time elapsed after the death of Villanueva and Ferdinand's return, before instructions were given to the architect Antonio López Aguado to reconstruct the building designated. Little information is available as to the progress of the works. Some attempt will be made, however, to clarify a few of its stages.

On 29 September 1816, Ferdinand took a second wife, his niece, Doña Isabella de Braganza, a Portuguese. Tradition regards this lady as the foundress of the Prado Museum. Eleven years after her death a picture was painted which represents her pointing to the edifice, the plans of which and suggestions for the arrangement of the works to be exhibited lie on a table before her. Don Pedro Beroqui, the learned historian of the Prado, has laboured to reduce Isabella's part in the affair to reasonable proportions. The Queen's early death on 26 December 1818, scarcely permits the attribution to her of anything more than intercession with the King in favour of the project. This view is well supported in a semi-official article published in the *Gazette* of 3 March 1818, the main points of which are underlined in the following extracts.

'The state into which the magnificent Science Museum has fallen as the result of a destructive war . . . has been a continual eyesore to the King . . . it has led him to conceive the noble aim of completing a structure which ... will eventually constitute one of the most splendid monuments in Madrid.

'His Majesty is persuaded that ... *Science and Art would gain by being once more united in this great masterpiece of architecture ...* As public funds cannot be applied to the execution of this project ... the building would soon fall into ruin if the King's own hand did not come to support it ... *His Majesty has decided to attend personally to the completion of an establishment of such importance. His pleasure in the undertaking has been increased by the Queen's generous offer to assist him in the work ...* His Majesty has accordingly resolved to begin by finishing the section intended to house the Gallery of Fine Art. He plans to transfer to it a number of the valuable paintings which at present adorn the royal palaces. In this way the pictures will be well preserved, available for study by the teaching staff and a source of pleasure to the public.'

In view of the above evidence Ferdinand VII cannot be deprived of the distinction of having established the Museum, though it is the only bright spot in his character.


*Management by the Grandees of Spain*

A document of unknown date, but earlier than 24 February 1818, records that the Marquis of Santa Cruz, Adviser to the Royal Academy of Fine Art, has been instructed by the King to 'furnish the Picture Gallery of the Prado Museum with paintings belonging to His Majesty'. Naturally enough, the principal Court Painter, Vicente López, assisted the Marquis in his task.

On 4 February 1819, the King paid a visit to the Museum and inspected the pictures undergoing restoration.

A few months later constructional work was expedited, even the usual Sunday's rest being dispensed with, in order to have the building ready for opening, if possible, on the occasion of the King's third marriage. On 20 October this year he married Marie Josèphe Amelia of Saxony. On 12 November the two thousand items of the catalogue drawn up by Don Luis Eusebi, curator of the establishment and painter of mediocre ability, were installed. On 19 November the Museum was thrown open to the public. At that time no one was aware of the painful road which had led to its establishment, nor could anyone then have dreamed of the astonishing treasures which would one day be displayed in the building.

The infant Gallery contained three hundred and eleven paintings, hung in the first floor rooms adjoining the rotunda. Pictures by Spanish artists, from Juan de Juanes and Sánchez Coello to those recently deceased, such as Paret and Francisco Bayeu, as well as some works by living painters like Goya, Aparicio and José de Madrazo, were exhibited both in the rooms on the right, today containing examples of the Northern Schools of the fifteenth and sixteenth centuries and also in the left-hand rooms, now devoted to Italian painting, as well as in the front hall, at present occupied by the Spanish Primitives. There were numerous works by Velasquez and Murillo, each being represented by forty-three, and several paintings of the school of Velasquez. It is disconcerting to find that the number of still-life studies by Luis Meléndez reached the same figure. Twenty-eight items were by Ribera, while fifteen were attributed to Juan de Juanes. Goya's portraits of Charles IV and Queen Maria Luisa were on view.

The Marquis of Santa Cruz, who had worked so energetically for the opening of the Museum, left Madrid on 21 March 1820 for Paris, where he had been appointed ambassador. But he continued to take an interest in the restoration of pictures from Aranjuez and La Granja, which were to be hung in another room of the building. His brother-in-law, the Prince of Anglona, succeeded him as Director of the Museum, proving a brilliant manager. The catalogue of 1821 lists as many as five hundred and twelve items, the Italian School alone accounting for a hundred and ninety-four.

The original proposal had been for Natural Science to share the building with the Fine Arts and it does not seem that this idea had been definitely abandoned. Two circumstances indicate that the accommodation was in fact shared. Negatively, no written or printed

VICENTE LOPEZ *Self-portrait*

statements allude to the presence of pictures on the ground floor, which may therefore have been devoted to other purposes. Positively, though here the evidence is rather slender, an enormous oval wooden box was still preserved some years ago in the storage premises at the Prado. It had a glass top in a gilt frame and contained 'naturalistic models of birds' perched on the branches of trees, such as are to be seen in some natural history museums. These objects had been so eaten away by maggots that they fell to dust as soon as the glass case was moved. But their existence proves that no immediate decision was taken to reserve the Prado accommodation for the arts only.

Modern ideas of curatorship soon began to penetrate the Prado. In 1823 a catalogue was published in French to encourage foreign visitors. This step was taken when a French army under the Duc d'Angoulême entered Spain to restore the royal despotism. The force under his command was known as the 'Hundred Thousand Sons of St Louis'. The catalogue in question includes for the first time Goya's *Mounted Bullfighter*.

The Prince of Anglona did not hold his position very long. Political changes led to his departure for Italy and he was succeeded on 27 December 1823 by the Marquis of Ariza. The respectable portraitist Vicente López, Principal Court Painter, was appointed Artistic Director.

Shortly afterwards some alterations were undertaken at the Museum: it was accordingly closed to the public from 31 March 1826. But a disagreement arose between Ariza and López with regard to the hanging arrangements proposed by the latter. The Marquis then approached the King directly, requesting him to nominate some person of equal rank to act for the Director during his absence. At the same time he added that 'in view of his personal knowledge of the institution and the circumstances of its foundation' he did not favour the alterations which the Court Painter wished to carry out. 'They are,' Ariza observed, 'personal fancies of his own, for the present arrangement is much admired by the teaching staff, by other intelligent persons and by the most distinguished of our foreign visitors. The funds required for such modifications would be better employed in restoration of the paintings themselves, which still remains to be undertaken.'

Ferdinand, who was at Seville, appointed the Duke of Híjar to replace Ariza during the latter's absences. The King also ordered, on 3 May 1826, 'the alterations projected by Vicente López to be postponed until Híjar authorizes the works'. Eleven days later the painter submitted to the King's instructions, remarking that there was no point in postponing the planned rearrangements, as 'the work has not yet started'.

Ariza did not resume his post. Hijar was the last Grandee of Spain to manage the affairs of the Prado. He did so successfully for twelve years. It was he who chose the pictures and statues to be transferred to the Prado from the various royal palaces. He also developed a logical arrangement of them, which differed from that of López, at the Museum. On his instructions the Spanish School was to occupy the rooms on each side of the rotunda. Works by living artists were to be hung in the vestibule of the gallery devoted to Italian painting. In the rear rotunda, where Goya's pictures are today displaced, the French and German Schools were to be installed. On the completion of the apartments designed to flank the rotunda, Flemish paintings were to be housed in those sections.

In 1826 the first floor contained, apart from the accommodation mentioned above, only the rest-room, which was at that time reserved for royal visitors, but which today houses works by Tiepolo. The perpendicular wing at the centre of the gallery, now the Velasquez Room, did not exist at that period. Accordingly, the arrangement made by the Duke of Hijar was perfectly suitable.

In this same year the Academy had to return the pictures it had been keeping since 1816, as well as the famous 'nudes', which had been in its custody much longer, stored in a private room. The transfer was confirmed by a royal order. But the King, by a decree in his own handwriting, warned Hijar that he expressly forbade 'the exhibition to the public of the indecent pictures stored in the said private rooms'. One wonders what Philip II would have thought of this order by his puritanical descendant. The paintings in question were brought to the Prado on 5 April 1827. They were not shown to the public during the whole reign of Ferdinand VII.

The Museum was reopened, after its reorganization by Hijar, on 19 March 1828, the Queen's birthday. Eusebi produced a catalogue fuller than any of its predecessors, listing seven hundred and fifty-seven items. He also enlarged it with critical notes and biographies of the living artists. A typical example of his judgment is the note

ALVAREZ DE SOTOMAYOR *Duke of Hijar*

on Tiepolo's *Immaculate Conception,* where he remarks: 'Agreeable colour. The treatment of drapery somewhat resembles that of Albrecht Dürer.' An equally extraordinary observation relates to the *Forge of Vulcan:* 'The figure of Vulcan conveys the impression that the poison of jealousy is circulating beneath his skin, through the livid black blood.'

Hijar also took pains to improve the exterior of the building, adorning it with sculpture. He decorated the interior with statues, including bronzes by Leoni, from the royal palaces. The Duke's period of office was in fact a most important one in the history of the Prado.

One of its most curious and typical episodes took place as a result of the death on 29 September 1833 of Ferdinand VII, the founder and protector of the institution.

Philip VI, in his Will, dated 14 September 1665, had declared inalienable 'in order that they may remain an integral part of Crown property ... all the paintings, writing-desks and porphyry urns'. Charles II had extended this disposition to cover other articles and Philip V had followed suit. But Charles III had considered that only the jewels should be regarded as inalienable and that other personal property could be transferred. Most fortunately, this clause of his Will was ignored, at both his own death and that of Charles IV. Yet it was taken into account on the decease of Ferdinand VII. Two daughters survived him. An inventory was therefore drawn up of the pictures, statues, bronzes and so on, their value being estimated at 38,873,279 *reals,* this figure covering the paintings, sculptures and panels in the Prado. It was deemed practicable to divide the items in question between the two sisters!

The execution of the plan was postponed until Isabella II came of age. A juridical committee then reasonably enough concluded that it had been a mistake to include in the inventory 'works reflecting past national glories and power, at all times owned by the kings of Spain. The idea of distributing such monuments cannot be contemplated without repugnance.' A year later, on 17 May 1845, the same committee advised the Queen, in order to retain intact a collection handed down to her through the centuries, to indemnify her sister in cash to the value of three-quarters of the property that would otherwise have fallen to her share. If this rational solution of the question had not been accepted, one trembles to think of what would have happened to the items allotted to the Queen's sister. At the same time it is only fair to stress the fact that this patriotic but not strictly just settlement involved considerable hardship to the Queen's collateral relatives.

The Prado, accordingly, was managed by Grandees of Spain for twenty years. Little documentary evidence is available as to the efficiency of their control. Two books dealing with this matter have been published, Beroqui's *Prado Museum: Notes for a History* of which only the first volume, entitled *The Royal Museum 1819–1833*, appeared in Madrid in 1933, and Madrazo's *History of the Prado Museum 1818–1868*, issued at Madrid in 1945. These works express different opinions as to the parts played in the management of the institution by the painters employed, and by the curators, who were not professional artists. My own view is simply that the solid foundation laid for the subsequent influence of the Prado was due both to the initial energy of the Marquis of Santa Cruz and the loyalty and good management of the Duke of Hijar, as well as to the practical knowledge and good sense of Vicente López and the labours of Luis Eusebi, Keeper, artist and editor of the catalogue.

*Committee of Management of the Royal Museum*

During the regency of the Queen-Mother, Maria Christina de Bourbon, on behalf of Isabella II as a minor, the Museum began to free itself from Palace control. On 20 June 1836, a Committee of Management of the Royal Museum was formed. It consisted of the Court Chamberlain, none other than the Duke of Hijar, and three officials of the Royal Household, two of whom were Court Painters and the third a sculptor. Their names were respectively Vicente López, José de Madrazo and Francisco Elias.

The Committee undertook the organization of the Second Sculpture Room. In 1837 Madrazo, though a painter, was engaged on the catalogue of that section. Born in 1781, he had been in the service of Charles IV in Rome. Ferdinand VII had appointed him, on 10 November 1816, Painter in Ordinary to the King. Thereafter, in collaboration with Vicente López, he participated in the establishment of the Prado. Together with Ramon Castilla he founded the Royal Lithographic Institute. A royal order of 21 March 1825, conferred on him the privilege, for ten years, of reproducing the pictures in the Museum and the royal palaces. In 1826 the first volume of the magnificent *Lithographic Collection of the Pictures of the King of Spain* appeared. Its preliminary pages contain a description by the architect López Aguado of the Prado building, which by then included the Lithographic Studio. The outbreak of the first civil war on 2 March 1837, prevented the issue of further volumes of the *Collection*. Its fifth section had just been published.

The talents of José de Madrazo were sufficiently numerous, and his services more than adequate, for recognition to be granted him on the reorganization of the Museum. Accordingly, when a royal decree of 12 April 1838, ended the functions of the Committee of Management, relieved the institution of administration by the Palace and provided for the appointment of a Curator responsible for the internal management of the building, José de Madrazo, on 21 April was nominated to the post.

The first year of his service was notable for certain innovations, in particular changes in the days and hours of admission of the public. Sundays and holidays were substituted for Wednesdays and Saturdays. The new hours were from eight in the morning till two in the afternoon from May to October, and from ten to three during the rest of the year. On 6 September, a royal visit lasting four hours took place. Plans were drawn up for the opening of new rooms. Royal permission was obtained on 29 December for custody by the Prado of the jewels constituting the 'Dauphin's Treasure'. After being returned by the French Government they had been displayed in the Natural History Department as specimens of minerals! Finally,

*José de Madrazo*

on 29 January 1839, Madrazo requested the transfer to the Museum of forty-eight pictures from the Escorial. This step was justified by the alarm caused through the extension of the Civil War.

Madrazo's new duties were not very congenial to him according to a letter in the book by his great-grandson mentioned above. A few days before his appointment he wrote: 'The rumour is all over Madrid that I shall be given this post and I can tell you that it is not going to afford me the slightest satisfaction, above all at this moment, when I am as full of enthusiasm as when I was a child. I wouldn't change places with an emperor when I've brushes in my hand.' He had the good sense to add that if the post had been exclusively concerned with art he would have been glad to accept it, but unfortunately that was not so, since it entailed certain other obligations and responsibilities.

But his abilities were such that he remained for a long time at the head of the Museum, where his management was most effective.

He established six new rooms in the building. They were opened on 27 April 1839. A further catalogue was also issued. As Luis Eusebi had died on 26 August 1828, Madrazo assigned its preparation to José Musso y Valiente, who had collaborated in the text which accompanied the *Lithographic Collection*. But Musso y Valiente died before he had done more than compose the notes to the Flemish and Dutch collections. Madrazo then passed the work to his son Pedro, a distinguished author and historian.

The catalogue was not completed until 21 October 1843, when it ran to four hundred and fifty-eight pages, dealing with one thousand nine hundred and forty-nine paintings, of which a hundred and one came from the Escorial. The book continued to be revised, with additions and modifications, until 1910.

Madrazo also paid attention to the exterior of the building. In 1842 he put up the large relief decorating the main frontage. In 1845 work was begun on the wing running east from the centre of the edifice, the most imposing portion of the structure, which Chueca had compared, in his analysis of Villanueva's plans, with a basilica prolonged by its apse. A drawing by José Avrial shows this wing long before it was completed. According to Beroqui the approved scheme anticipated completion on 14 December 1847. But in fact it was not until 1853 that the Museum was closed from 19 January to 13 May the latter date being that of the conclusion of the work. The new structure was not divided into floors. A gallery ran round the interior at first floor height containing, like the famous Tribune of the Uffizi Gallery at Florence, specially selected paintings. From this gallery a view was obtained of the well of the hall, where sculpture was exhibited. The apartment as a whole was called the Isabella II Room. On 18 April it was visited by the Queen and her husband. When the Museum reopened, the entire building, as planned by Villanueva, had at last been constructed.

No further developments worth mentioning took place until 1857. By that time the Palace finances were in a sorry state owing to the enormous sums borrowed on the security of Crown property, and the Comptroller of the Household considered that the Museum should also exercise due economy.

Its management, responsible for the restoration of the pictures, had created a complete studio to undertake this work, whereas in the Comptroller's opinion restoration should consist simply of an 'inspection by the authorities with a view to taking moderate, sober and conscientious steps for the preservation and restoration of such pictures as, in the judgement of the Director and after due information imparted to and consent obtained from Her Majesty, should undergo repairs, work which must, with good reason, excite apprehension'. In reality Madrazo had already substituted restoration by varnishing for the harmful use of oil for this purpose. Years later he wrote that pictures should never be subjected to overmuch cleaning 'so that they may retain their glazing and the venerable patina of age'. This advice is in line with Goya's admirable remark that 'time, too, paints'.

The measures of economy decreed by the Marquis of Santa Isabel, the Comptroller, involving a reduction of the staff and interference with the internal administration of the Museum, were resented by Madrazo. A long dispute ensued. It ended, on 30 March 1857, with the resignation of the Curator, which was accepted. He withdrew from direction of the Museum, but remained Court Painter.

On 26 May, Juan Antonio Ribera, who had recently retired from the office of Court Painter, was appointed Director of the Museum. Federigo de Madrazo, who had been Second Court Painter to the King since 1850, protested energetically against this appointment, considering he had a better right to it than Ribera. He submitted a memorandum resigning his official post. But this petition was rejected. On 15 June he was nominated First Painter in Ordinary.

Ribera remained responsible for the Museum until his death, which occurred on 15 June 1860. His term of office did no particular harm or good to the Prado. He confined his activities to maintenance of the structure and restoration of the paintings.

On 19 July in the same year Federigo de Madrazo succeeded Ribera. Federigo, an artist of considerable merit, excelled in portraiture. He also knew a great deal about the history of painting and gave valuable information and advice to his brother Pedro for the improvement of the catalogue. His first activities as Director – for he subsequently returned to the office for a longer period – were administratively successful, all the departments being efficiently reorganized.

The ceiling of the Queen's Reception Room, which had been painted by Vicente, was transferred in 1866 to the Prado, being placed in the rest-room reserved for royal visits, where works by Tiepolo are now displayed. The large Sèvres vase presented to Isabella II in 1865 by Napoleon III and the Empress Eugénie was installed in the room containing the 'Dauphin's Treasure'. Orders were given for the conveyance to the Museum of Goya's designs for tapestry and 'fourteen panels of the School of van Eyck depicting the life of Our Lord', forming part of the altarpiece painted by Juan de Flandes and Miguel Sitium for Queen Isabella I. But this last order was never carried out. Nor were two pictures by Goya in the Prince's House at the Escorial ever taken to the Prado as directed. But these instructions and the transfers mentioned are a proof of the strenuous efforts made by Madrazo to increase the Prado collections.

Isabella II bought a few pictures, though without showing much discrimination. They added little to the value of the works in the Museum. Almost all of them were eventually sent to Aranjuez or Riofrio. Ever since the time of Isabella the Catholic, and possibly in that of her brother and father, the Spanish sovereigns had been interested in and patronized the fine arts. This remarkable chain of continuity, to which painting in general owes so much, was broken in the case of Isabella II.

*Isabella II*

The Prado collections, by this time very extensive and for the most part on exhibition, were admired not only by persons particularly fond of pictures and by professional artists. By 1807 the influx of visitors was causing quite a problem, proving the interest taken by the citizens of Madrid in the Museum. It is stated that at a later period the crowds on Sundays were so great that 'they could not be kept moving' and four veterans of the Civil Guard had to be called in to control the situation. This clearly shows the Museum's popularity.

The reign of Isabella II was one of the most troubled in the history of Spain. Revolution broke out on 29 September 1868. The Queen fled to France. This event gave rise to further developments of great consequence for the Prado. Comments by Madrazo, recorded in his great-grandson's book, show how deeply he was affected by these changes. In one particularly moving passage he writes: 'Artists should have united in calling the attention of the Assembly to the necessity of continuing the services provided by the Museum, so as to prevent political events from affecting it adversely and causing it to be closed to artists and the public. But nothing of the kind is being done. What a calamity!'

On 19 November 1868, Madrazo resigned. Both the Statute establishing the Museum and its very name were about to be altered.

As stated above, the lawyers charged with the interpretation of the Will of Ferdinand VII had declared that the Prado Museum constituted part of the property legally divisible between Isabella II and her sister. But they had advised the Queen to compensate her sister in cash rather than permit a partition of these artistic treasures. On 12 May 1865, however, a law was passed including the Royal Museum of Painting and Sculpture, together with the Royal Palace and the Arsenal, among the items of indivisible property appertaining to the Crown, but not providing for any indemnity to the co-heiress for the loss of her share.

When the revolution succeeded, it was only logical to proceed further. A law dated 9 and 18 December 1869, decreed the extinction of the royal patrimony and the return to the State of all the property which had composed it, with the exception of 'items intended for the use and service of the King'. For Spain was still a monarchy, though it no longer had a monarch. The list of exceptions, however, did not comprise, among other missing items, the Royal Museum. It was thus, though without explicit statement of the fact, nationalized.

The first Director under the new conditions was Antonio Gisbert. The post of Deputy Director was created for the sculptor José Gragera. Both men possessed the confidence of the Government. In 1872 Gisbert moved his office into the rest-room formerly reserved for royal visitors.

The Museum was not immediately placed under State control. Official documents continued to bear the heading 'Royal Museum' for some time afterwards. On 22 February 1870, the Ministry of Culture claimed the right of jurisdiction in the Museum's affairs from the Ministry of Finance. In a bulletin of 16 March His Highness the Regent conceded this right under certain specified conditions. It was implied that the costs of maintenance would be borne by the Ministry of Culture. But, as always happens in such cases, the office originally in charge of the administration of property formerly belonging to the Crown continued to meet the expenses of the Museum for a few months longer.

*Union with the Trinidad Museum*

During these troubled years many anxieties precluded normal initiative in the field of art. But one important step was taken. The Prado became associated with the National Museum of Painting and Sculpture, generally called the 'Trinidad Museum', from the name of the monastery which it occupied. The title of 'National', however, had been assumed by the Prado Museum as soon as it ceased to be 'Royal'. This fact should be borne in mind, as it has given rise to much misunderstanding, in Spain itself as well as abroad.

The Trinidad Museum had been established on 13 January 1836. It housed the paintings removed from the monasteries suppressed in the Provinces of Madrid, Toledo, Avila and Segovia. A royal order of 31 December 1837, had assigned it accommodation in the Trinitarian Monastery, Atocha Street.

On 24 July 1838, the new museum assumed the title of 'National', which at the time caused no confusion with the still existent Royal Museum. It was also distinguished from the Prado by the fact that it contained a section devoted to contemporary art, in which the pictures had all been bought by private negotiation or at recent exhibitions.

Yet the Trinidad Museum was really no such thing. Its former Deputy Director, Gregorio Cruzada Villamil, wrote in his provisional catalogue published in 1865: 'As the pictures are today distributed among the various rooms and offices of the Ministry of Culture' – for the Ministry had also moved into the huge, dilapidated monastery – 'they cannot be classified, and hung as an exhibition to be shown to the public.' It was hoped that they would ultimately be transferred to the palace being built in the Recoletos Avenue to accommodate both the Library and the national museums.

José Echegaray, head of the Ministry of Culture, did his best to remedy this deplorable state of affairs. He was a cultivated, intelligent man, destined, thirty-five years later, to be awarded a Nobel Prize for literature. In a decree issued by the Provisional Government on 25 November 1870, he appointed a committee to investigate the possibility of combining the two Museums. The initial phrases of the preamble may raise a smile. They read: 'The famous panels of van Eyck and Rincón and the canvases painted by Rivera [sic], Morales and Murillo should be kept together and exhibited for the admiration of both Spaniards and foreigners.' It may be observed that in reality Spain has never possessed any work by van Eyck, that the second name mentioned may have been intended by the future dramatist for one Antonio Ricón, though no pictures by this person are known, that Ribera's name is spelt with a 'b' and finally that Morales hardly ever painted on canvas.

Like all new regimes the Provisional Government of Spain flung itself recklessly into vast schemes. Plans were laid to constitute the enormous, projected museum by collecting works belonging to the State and dispersed among such institutions as the Archaeological Museum, provincial galleries, churches, the premises of various corporations and even the St Ferdinand Academy. It may be wondered where such a multitude of works of art could be housed. 'It is true,' answers Echegaray, 'that the Prado building is not yet big enough to contain all the items in its possession. But the Constituent Assembly has granted the Government, in the Budget of this year, a permanent credit of 200,000 *pesetas* for the enlargement of the edifice. Although this sum falls short of the amount required for the adequate housing of the works belonging to the two museums, it will be enough to ensure that of the best items in each collection.' Official optimism went even further. It was announced that a Museum of Contemporary Art would shortly be established.

The actual incorporation of the Trinidad collection with that of the Prado took place only in consequence of a decree of 22 March 1872. Although the Trinidad possessed a very large number of pictures, they were not all of the highest quality. Most were by Spanish artists. The panels of the fifteenth and sixteenth centuries supplied by the Trinidad filled a gap. Seventeenth-century Spanish and Italian paintings were stored by the Prado authorities in certain public buildings, such as the universities, the Supreme Court of Appeal, some churches and a few law-courts. Several provincial galleries also benefited. These transfers were made in a spirit very different from that of modern times. It was consequently necessary at a later date to obtain the restitution of certain works judged to be indispensable for the completion of the Prado collections.

Some of the most important of these were Maino's *Adoration of the Kings*, Carreño's *St Sebastian*, the *Apotheosis of St Augustine* by Claudio Coello, Goya's *Christ*, the *Virgin of the Catholic Monarchs*, the *Fountain of Grace* in the style of the van Eycks, the great triptych of the *Redemption* by van der Weyden, the *Transfiguration* after Raphael, and Giovanni Domenico Tiepolo's *Passion* series.

The proclamation of the First Republic, on 2 February 1873, brought no great changes in the management and activities of the Prado. Mariano de Madrazo reports that the Minister of Culture, Joaquin Gil Berges, offered the post of Director to Federigo de Madrazo who, however, replied that 'he did not consider it his duty to accept' the position. During the administration of President Castelar a decree was countersigned by Berges containing two remarkable innovations, both indicative of his personality. In the first place, the Museum was to publish an annual bulletin listing its acquisitions and exchange transactions. 'The bulletin will include', the decree stated, 'monographs written by eminent artists and critics on the most notable pictures and statues possessed by the Museum.' In the second place, 'By agreement with the Academy of Fine Art a series of public lectures will be arranged to deal with questions of aesthetics, criticism and the history of fine art.' These high-minded ideas were put forward much too early to stand any chance of accomplishment. The Republic had only seven weeks more to live at the date of this decree, which accordingly remained a dead letter.

On the collapse of the regime Antonio Gisbert, who had been appointed Director on 21 November 1868, was obliged to resign. His successor was a now forgotten painter, Francisco Sanz y Cabo.

Evidence of the stability of the Museum during this troubled period is provided by its catalogues. When the revolution of 1868 broke out, the first volume – the only one published – of the *Descriptive and Historical Catalogue* was being printed. It had been edited, like previous catalogues since 1843, by Pedro de Madrazo. Page 252 is headed 'Royal Museum', while page 254 bears the heading 'Prado Museum'.

The same editor signed the 1873 catalogue. With admirable good sense he refers to the Museum simply as the 'Prado Museum'.

*New Title: The Prado*

The return of King Alfonso XII introduced an era of peace and stability, in which the Museum was enabled to make further progress. The unassuming Sanz y Cabo remained Director until his death on 5 May 1881. On 14 May Federigo de Madrazo was reappointed to the position, which he held until 10 June 1894. His tenure of the office therefore lasted, in two stages, thirty-one years.

In 1881 alteration of the north front was under consideration. Suñol was commissioned to execute a group to crown it. A further important transformation proposed was to reduce the level of the ground adjacent to the building so as to meet the base of the walls

*Federigo de Madrazo*

of both the north front and that portion of the east front facing San Jeronimo. The idea of freeing the ground floor from such close contact with the humidity of the soil was reasonable enough. But technical objections were advanced. In 1882 the architect Francisco Jareño was asked to prepare plans, which he submitted in November 1883. The work carried out in consequence was modified in 1942 by the architect Pedro de Muguruza in order to provide direct entry to the ground floor rotunda.

Restoration of the roofing of the Isabella II Room was begun by Jareño and completed by Eduardo de Saavedra, Engineer for Roads and Bridges and Director of the Royal Academy of History.

Four editions of the catalogue were printed during the reign of Alfonso XII and three during the regency of Maria Christina. The last of the series appeared in 1901, after the death of the editor, Pedro de Madrazo, which occurred on 20 August 1898.

His brother Federigo had died four years before the Isabella II Room, after the expensive transformation of its roofing, was ready for use. Advantage had been taken of the works to eliminate the gallery overlooking the ground floor and also to divide the room into two storeys by a ceiling fitted at the height of the first floor.

THE TWENTIETH CENTURY

## Finishing Touches to the Museum

Three Directors followed Madrazo in a short space of time. Vicente Palmaroli died on 24 January 1896. Francisco Padilla was appointed on 3 February of that year and resigned on 29 July 1898. His successor, Luis Alvarez, died on 4 October 1901. All three men were painters, highly respected and popular at the period, but their terms of office were too brief to enable them to influence the development of an institution in which progress can only be achieved by prolonged and continuous work.

The centenary of the birth of Velasquez was commemorated by an exhibition of his works in the Isabella II Room, where they are still hung. The idea was due to Aureliano de Beruete y Moret, a landscape painter and critic, who had specialized in the study of the great Sevillan. As President of the Committee de Beruete delivered the opening address on 6 June 1899. On the same day a seated statue of the illustrious artist, the work of Aniceto Marinas, was unveiled in front of the main entrance to the Museum. On this occasion the Duke of San Fernando presented the Prado with the larger *Christ on the Cross* of Velasquez, while the Duchess of Villahermosa added his portraits of Don Diego del Corral and his wife.

Luis Alvarez was succeeded by José de Villegas, till then Director of the Spanish Academy of Fine Art on the Janiculum Hill in Rome. Villegas remained in charge of the Museum until 18 December 1918. He organized three notable exhibitions at the Prado during his term of office; they were devoted to the works of El Greco in 1902, to those of Zurbarán in 1905 and to those of Morales in 1917. The Deputy Director, Salvador Viniegra, collaborated ably with Villegas and from 1910 onwards the institution was served by a Secretary of exceptional talents, Pedro Beroqui. A lawyer employed by the Government, Beroqui had studied the history of painting in association with the indefatigable and learned José Marti Monso of Valladolid. The former's expert knowledge of ancient records enabled him to throw new light on the history of the Museum and that of many of the pictures in the collection. He died on 16 July 1955, aged 88.

91

José de Villegas *Self-portrait*

During the Directorship of Villegas a decision of extreme importance for the development of the Museum was taken. A royal decree, countersigned on 7 June 1912 by Santiago Alba, created a Board of Patronage consisting of collectors, critics, art historians and professional artists under the chairmanship of the Duke of Alba. The Board at first concentrated on taking the most urgent measures required to bring the Prado into line with the other great European galleries. It was decided to increase the number of rooms to twenty-two, those of the first floor being provided with top lighting, without disturbing Villanueva's structure. Fernando Arbos carried out the work.

Simultaneously with the undertaking of these substantial alterations, the Board, at the suggestion of my own teacher, the erudite scholar Don Elias Tormo (d. 1957), professor of the history of art, ordered the inventories of the royal palaces, preserved in the archives of the Palace of Madrid, to be copied and studied, with a view to discovering the history of every picture mentioned. This task was entrusted to me in October 1913. The subsequent history of the Museum is derived to a large extent from my personal recollections, at first those of a mere witness, later those of a participant and even at times of a protagonist. I shall try, however, to give an objective account of these events.

As regards the structure itself, works of enlargement were undertaken between 1914 and 1920. Two courtyards on the San Jeronimo side, between the North and South Sections and the central portion of the building, known as the Velasquez Room, were closed.

In September 1918 some of the jewels in the 'Dauphin's Treasure' were stolen, while others were in need of repair. In consequence a dispute arose in October between the Board and the Directorate. José de Villegas and José Garnelo, Deputy Director since 1914, resigned. The Board recommended to the Minister of Education and Fine Art that their places should be taken by Aureliano de Beruete y Moret and Fernando Alvarez de Sotomayor. These gentlemen were accordingly appointed on 31 December.

De Beruete was the son of the painter and critic already mentioned. A collector and member of the Board of Patronage, he was the author of some first-rate monographs, one of which dealt with Goya in three volumes published between 1916 and 1918. De Sotomayor was an eminent painter who had studied in Rome. At the request of the Government of Chile he had successfully established the School of Fine Art in that country. This was the first occasion on which a writer who was not a professional artist had been placed in charge of the Prado.

On 1 January 1919, a small committee consisting of my friend and collaborator Juan Allende-Salazar and myself began regular editorial work on the catalogue.

He had a most detailed knowledge of the history of painting, being one of the best informed of Spaniards on the subject. But his precarious health and early death prevented him from writing the works which might reasonably have been expected from him. We both worked in close association with Pedro Beroqui, who published an edition of the catalogue in the following year. His excessive personal modesty and respect for the previous editor, Pedro de Madrazo, caused him to retain the latter's name as responsible editor.

The rapid progress of the works of enlargement enabled new rooms to be opened in 1920, containing French paintings, those of El Greco and those in which the larger *Christ on the Cross* of Velasquez and his landscapes of the Villa Medici were hung.

In the spring of 1922 paintings began to be installed in the Rubens Room. On 10 June, Beruete, who had long been ill, died at the age of only forty-five. Alvarez de Sotomayor succeeded him, and to my great astonishment I was myself appointed Deputy Director, a post which I held until 1960 when I became Director.

At that time our next task was to transform and decorate the large Velasquez Room. Beruete had been in the habit of taking quick decisions. But at the time of his death he had still not made any plans or at any rate any definite arrangements for the reconstitution of the room in question.

Before the end of the year 1922 the Museum's staff was strengthened by the eminent architect Pedro de Muguruza, who planned and directed all the construction work until 1942, and the learned professor and academician Diego Angulo, who took my place on the Catalogue Committee.

I do not think I need chronicle the alterations carried out in all the Rooms of the Prado. I shall therefore confine myself to noting the most important of them. These included the building, in 1926, of a staircase adjoining the Velasquez Room, the protection in 1927 of the central gallery by a lining of reinforced cement, the installation in 1928 of Goya's designs for tapestry, the construction of a staircase and rooms on the third floor of the North Section during 1929/30, and finally in 1930 works for the Fernandez-Duran Bequest.

Three large exhibitions were organized at this period. In 1927 the International Exhibition of copper engravings from Rome, Paris and Madrid was held under the auspices of the International Museums Office. In 1928 a splendid exhibition commemorated the centenary of Goya's death. In 1929 the second centenary of the birth of Mengs was similarly celebrated.

These events furnished the occasions for publication of two detailed catalogues. That dealing with the Goya exhibition was edited by Enrique Lafuente, who had the advantage of notes and recommendations by Allende-Salazar. I myself edited the Mengs catalogue.

As there was no friction whatever between the Board of Patronage, the directing staff and the architect, a continuous programme of improvements on a soundly planned basis could be undertaken. These were all supported by the various Governments and facilitated by the special interest of King Alfonso XIII in the Museum, an attitude inherited from his family. Unfortunately the constitutional change of April 1931 caused a temporary suspension of the works in hand. The Director resigned, and was replaced in May by Ramon Perez de Ayala, the novelist and essayist, who was at the same time appointed Ambassador of the Republic in London. It was not until five years later, after he had ceased to exercise his diplomatic functions, that Ayala became actively concerned in the direction of the Museum. Even then he only held the post for three months, during a period of much agitation in Madrid.

Between 1931 and 1936 I had the honour and the heavy responsibility of duties both as Deputy Director and acting Director of the Prado. Throughout these five years I was loyally supported by the Board of Patronage, still under the chairmanship of the Duke of Alba. I could also count on the collaboration of my model Secretary, Pedro Beroqui, and on the technical advice of the architect Pedro de Muguruza. By our united efforts the hanging of the Fernandez-Duran Bequest was completed in June 1931 and the drawings by Goya were also satisfactorily placed in position. Meanwhile work continued on the splendid ground floor rotunda, which was opened in November 1934 at the same time as the Museums Congress organized by the International Museums Office of the Institute of Intellectual Co-operation of the League of Nations. A storeroom with metal fittings was constructed in 1935.


## The Revolution of 1936

Perez de Ayala had only been Director of the Museum in practice for a few weeks when the Nationalist rising took place. Rioting began in Madrid on 18 July 1936, followed almost at once by civil war. The Museum remained open until 30 August.

Early in September Perez de Ayala succeeded in escaping abroad. On 20 September the Government appointed Pablo Picasso Director. But he never assumed office and did not cross the threshold of the Museum. Though I was closely concerned with the matter I have never understood, from that day to this, why this appointment was made, apart from its possible value as propaganda.

The genius of Picasso and the part he has played in the evolution of art for half a century are indisputable. But during this troubled period it was with stupefaction that I learned, from a statement by this celebrated artist, that 'the Prado was being guarded by the heroic militia and it was necessary to await the triumph of the people before taking action'.

In due course I drew up a documented report of events at the Prado until the beginning of January 1938, when I was ordered to hand over my post to the architect and painter Roberto Fernandez Balbuena. In the present connection I am bound to record that ordinary citizens never made the slightest attempt to interfere with the Museum. The pictures were stacked in the most solidly roofed of the rooms and protected with sandbags.

At the beginning of November 1936 orders were received to forward the works of art to Valencia. I was most reluctant to do so. Transport and the possibility of eventual evacuation abroad would certainly expose these items to more risk than retaining them in Madrid. I was equally convinced that the Museum would not be intentionally attacked from the air and that if a bomb were dropped in the vicinity the precautions we had taken would most probably be sufficient to prevent disaster.

I therefore proceeded as slowly as possible in giving instructions for the despatch of the pictures, hoping that a cessation of the siege of the capital would soon render it unnecessary to face the hazards of removal. Five hundred and twenty-five paintings were eventually sent, together with some carefully selected Goya drawings and the jewels of the 'Dauphin's Treasure'.

*Reopening of the Museum: the Prado today*

Madrid fell on 28 March 1939. Two days later I was reappointed to my former post. Work was immediately begun on the cleaning and repair of the edifice, which I had tried to save from dilapidation during the civil war, in spite of the ridicule to which these efforts exposed me. I was told that 'the People', after their victory, would build an incomparably larger and finer Museum and that consequently it was a waste of time to stop up holes in the roofs and prevent the woodwork from rotting.

The work of repair was carried out with such enthusiasm that on 26 April the Minister of Education and other authorities were able to visit the Museum and examine all the works which had been stored away and were by then back in position once again. The first instalment of the pictures which had been evacuated had arrived on 15 April.

On 7 July 1939, the Prado reopened. It had been closed since 30 August 1936. Some pictures had still not yet been returned. Substitutes for the time being were borrowed from churches, monasteries and other museums which had been 'sequestrated or placed in protective custody'. No works, however, were borrowed from private owners. I gave the Catalogue of this exhibition a somewhat grandiose title: 'From Barnaba de Modena to Francisco de Goya. An Exhibition of Paintings from the Fourteenth to the Nineteenth

*F. J. Sánchez Cantón*

Century retrieved by Spain.'

At the same time a dazzling selection of pictures from the Museum and tapestries from the Palace was exhibited at Geneva under the management of Fernando Alvarez de Sotomayor. It had been suggested by the Prado Board of Patronage, the Chairman of which in Nationalist Spain was Count Romanones, Director of the St Ferdinand Royal Academy of Fine Art. This first loan of the most valuable treasures of the Museum was most warmly acclaimed throughout Europe.

But the international atmosphere was darkened, at the beginning of September, by declarations of war. It became necessary to close the exhibition at Geneva and return the works displayed to Madrid by train. They were carried on roundabout routes, with all lights in the coaches extinguished.

They all reached the capital safely, though Goya's *Shootings of 3rd May 1808,* suffered some slight damage and his *People of Madrid attacking the Mamelukes* rather more. But with these exceptions the decidedly hazardous Geneva enterprise was successfully concluded.

As soon as the Board of Patronage resumed its normal functions Alvarez de Sotomayor returned to the post of Director which he had occupied from June 1922 to April 1931, while I again became Deputy Director. The Museum was reconstituted on exactly the same lines as in July 1936.

The first work undertaken was the reconstruction of the staircase giving direct access to the ground floor rotunda. It was opened in 1942.

After a visit by the Head of the State in February of that year it was decided to replace the wooden ceilings and floors by paving and fire-resistant decorative features. The work, which proved costly and is still far from complete, has met with some criticism on the ground that the new paving is too hard and slippery. Whatever force there may be in this objection is disposed of by the advantages entailed: the stone is non-inflammable and eliminates the irritating echo of footsteps in rooms so crowded with visitors.

New accommodation was provided for the display of the 'Dauphin's Treasure' and of antique statues, of which the chief is the *Lady of Elche,* one of the items included, in return for pictures, drawings and a piece of tapestry, in a reciprocal arrangement with France that took place in 1941. Room was also found in this section for a considerable number of the sculptures presented in the same year by Señor Maria de Zayas, a Mexican citizen whose mother was Spanish.

At the beginning of 1953 the problem of enlarging the accommodation had to be faced. Various proposals were put forward. The plan eventually selected was that of the architects Manuel Lorente, official adviser to the Directorate of the Prado, and Fernando

Chueca, who had already been employed on works at the Museum. Their extremely simple and effective designs added sixteen rooms to the building, four being larger than the rest. In the garden area two structures were placed against those previously erected by Fernando Arbos, without disturbing the original edifice. The works were carried out with a rapidity which seems prodigious in view of the type of materials used, mostly granite and marble. Eleven months only were required, and this important annexe was opened on 9 June 1956. It enabled many pictures to be satisfactorily hung which had been for long invisible or badly placed. The collections on the ground and first floors of the Museum have accordingly been entirely rearranged and their classification much improved.

At this stage the brief history of the Prado here presented becomes a mere enumeration of facts. But these would not in themselves be sufficient without certain supplementary information.

On the death of Count Romanones in 1950 the illustrious author and former Minister, Señor Rafael Sanchez Mazas, was appointed Chairman of the Board of Patronage. Pedro de Muguruza, the architect who had supervised all works at the Museum from the autumn of 1922 to February 1952, retired in favour of his brother José Maria. The latter supervised the execution of the plans of Lorente and Chueca, undertook to renovate the Goya rotunda and drew up plans for the remodelling of the basement.

After the new rooms had been opened work was begun on the reconstruction of the south basement. Selected drawings and pastels are exhibited there, but the accommodation is also used for lectures. In the spring of 1958 three more new rooms were opened, one to contain British painting and the other two Flemish and Dutch.

In November of the same year the third-floor rooms of the North and South Sections were reorganized. They now contain part of the Flemish School, the Fernandez-Duran Bequest and the French School. Each Room also displays important items from the collection of drawings.

The Museum is now so flourishing and the promises of State aid so unequivocal that the question of alterations to the gallery constructed by Fernando Arbos has already been raised. The employment of non-inflammable materials and the transformation of its defective lighting are envisaged.

The gifts, bequests and purchases of the last sixty-five years are of little account in comparison with the treasures amassed by the kings of Spain and the contributions made by the Trinidad Museum. In former days Spain was a country of great religious and charitable institutions. But fewer patrons than might have been expected have appeared in modern times. The latest catalogues contain lists of donors of items to the Prado collections. But no more than seventy-two names are cited; moreover, the gifts themselves vary a good deal in quantity and quality. The items comprised in them are seldom both numerous and artistically outstanding.

In 1881 Baron Emile d'Erlanger presented to the Museum the fourteen astonishing paintings formerly in Goya's villa, most unsuitably known as his 'black works'. In 1904 Don Ramon de Errazy bequeathed to the Prado a roomful of pictures by Fortuny, Baudry, Ricardo Madrazo, Meissonier and Rico. The legacy was accepted in spite of the fact that some of the paintings overstepped the chronological limits laid down for the Prado collections, works executed after 1850 not being strictly eligible for exhibition. In 1915 Don Pablo Bosch bequeathed a fine set of pictures, both panels and canvases, including in particular admirable Flemish works of the fifteenth and sixteenth centuries. The legacy of Don Pedro Fernandez-Duran in 1930 comprised the works now exhibited in three splendid rooms, containing also tapestries, furniture and drawings. In addition to these important bequests the Museum also benefited from the wills of Luis de Errazu (1925), the Count of Niebla (1926), the Count of Cartagena (1930), the Duke of Tarifa (1934), Francisco Cambo (1940) and the Count of Muguiro (1946).

The list of works thus bequeathed, which could be extended, shows that more productions by Goya than by any other artist have recently been presented or left to the Prado. Nevertheless, examples of Flemish and Italian art have also considerably increased. On the other hand, Dutch and British works are few and far between. The royal collections had a certain influence on those in private ownership. Similar gaps and similar accumulations are found in both cases. Special gratitude is therefore due to the memory of Don Francisco Cambo for his bequest of Italian pictures of the fourteenth and fifteenth centuries. He had acquired these works with the deliberate intention of filling the gaps common to most Spanish collections.

Of purchases in recent times the first of any consequence was that of portraits of Goya and his wife, together with one hundred and eighty-six drawings, from the collection of Don Ramon de la Huerta. Two hundred and sixty-two other drawings had been bought at Cardereda in 1886. Others were found on the backs of several of the sheets: the Fernandez-Duran Bequest included nine. The self-portrait in ink was acquired by the Board of Patronage in 1945. A total of four hundred and eighty-three works in this category is thus computed.

The policy of the Board, ever since its creation, has been to concentrate on purchases which would fill gaps in the older collections. The bequest of the Count of Cartagena was a piece of good fortune from this point of view.

The Museum's own resources and the favour of the Minister of Education enabled the number of Spanish panels of the fifteenth and sixteenth centuries to be increased. Seven more pictures by El Greco and three more by Zurbarán, an artist more highly esteemed today than ever before, were acquired.

It has already been pointed out that the kings of Spain, doubtless for political reasons, made no effort to obtain Dutch paintings. But in recent times the Museum's desire to possess a few works of that School has led to the addition to its collection of a portrait by Scorel, a self-portrait by Rembrandt, the *Philosopher* by Salomon Koninck, landscapes by Hobbema and van Goyen, two portraits by Mierevelt and the *Adoration of the Shepherds* by Jacob Gerritsz Cuyp.

The British School, however, is still very poorly represented in the Prado. No picture of that School was listed in the palace inventories. The legacies of Don Luis de Errazu and the Duke of Arcos to the Museum included two portraits. But they are not of first-rate quality.

Two paintings by Reynolds have been bought, and one Gainsborough and one Lawrence were presented by Mr B. Newhouse of New York. Apart from works acquired in accordance with a preconceived plan, the Museum has always taken advantage of such casual opportunities as arose. It was in this way that three remarkable little pictures by Paret were purchased. He was an exact contemporary of Goya and dealt with subjects rather rare in Spanish painting, scenes of common life. Other interesting works similarly acquired are the *Portrait of a Gentleman* by Juan Bautista Maino, the *Hunting-party* of Juan Bautista del Mazo, a *St Augustine* by Mateo Carezo, Valdés Leal's *St Jerome and a Dignitary of his Order* and last but not least the austere and impressive portrait of *Sister Jeronima de la Fuente,* signed by Velasquez in 1620. With the *Adoration of the Kings* of 1619 and two male portraits, this work represents the Sevillan period of the master.

The above notes on the management, architectural modifications and collections of the Prado bring to an end this brief narrative of the chequered history of the Museum. Its perusal will have enabled the reader to realize that the Museum reflects the most characteristic features of Spanish life. The institution is the result of continuous activity subjected to a multiplicity of influences. Though the very antithesis of an improvised gallery, it is also far from having been organized on scientific lines by technicians who could count on ample funds. The Museum arose on a basis of constant, congenial and impassioned toil. It was spared the anxieties of bargaining and undue delays. Ten generations of sovereigns with a tradition of devotion to painting and fine discrimination in the art have been responsible for the establishment of the Prado. The Spanish kings had vast financial resources at their disposal as well as the expert advice of artists with whom they were in close touch. By the time that the Bourbons lost their rare endowment of artistic sensibility the Museum already belonged to the nation. Its improvement and enrichment thenceforth made splendid progress, reflecting the greatest credit on its Directors, the Board of Patronage and the Governments concerned.

# ITALIAN SCHOOL

## Fourteenth and Fifteenth Centuries

Fra Angelico (Giovanni da Fiesole), 1378–1455
*Annunciation (with the Expulsion from the Garden of Eden)*
Wood: 76³/₈ × 76³/₈ in. (194 × 194 cm.) Cat. 15

This detail forms part of an altarpiece consisting of a main panel and five smaller ones constituting the predella: the *Birth and Marriage of the Virgin, Visitation, Adoration of the Kings, Presentation in the Temple,* and *Death of the Virgin.*

The left side of the main panel, excluding the Brunelleschi-style loggia at which the Virgin receives the message from the archangel Gabriel, shows a delightful garden adorned with a variety of plants and flowers which the artist evidently enjoyed painting in the smallest detail. The size of this vegetation increases with its distance from the bottom of the picture. A citron-tree in full fruit and a palm are conspicuous. Adam and Eve, both clothed, are being driven in tears from the Garden by an angel who does not seem to be acting very violently. Adjacent mountains shut in the horizon. Above them the clouds part to admit a pencil of bright rays representing the descent of the Holy Ghost.

Fra Angelico's religious scruples would not permit him to exhibit Adam and Eve naked, as Masaccio had in the Brancacci Chapel of the Carmine at Florence. They are clothed in strict accordance with the Biblical text: 'Unto Adam also and to his wife did the Lord God make coats of skins

Fra Angelico *Adoration of the Kings*

and clothed them ... So he drove out the man; and he placed at the east of the Garden of Eden Cherubims and a flaming sword ... to keep the way of the Tree of Life.'

The panel was painted between 1430 and 1445 for the monastery of St Dominic at Fiesole. In 1611 the monks, in order to meet the cost of erecting a steeple, sold the picture to Duke Mario Farnese for the Duke of Lerma. It was placed in the Prado on 16 July 1861, having been obtained from the Descalzas Reales (Royal Barefoot Sisterhood) convent. In 1943 the panel was expertly cleaned and restored by the craftsmen of the Museum, with surprising results, especially in the case of the section here reproduced.

Professor A. L. Mayer attributed the very fine paintings on the predella to Zanobi Strozzi. But his opinion has not been generally accepted. Their merits are precisely such as are found elsewhere in the works of the master.

ANDREA MANTEGNA, 1431–1506 *Death of the Virgin*
Wood: 21¹/₄ × 16¹/₂ in. (54 × 42 cm.) Cat. 248

The Virgin is lying on her death-bed, attended by eleven Apostles holding wax candles. St Thomas is missing. According to the apocryphal work known as the 'Narrative of the Pseudo-Arimatheus', with which the iconography of the subject agrees, Thomas had been on a mission to India and arrived late on the scene.

The architecture of the chamber is classical, its pilasters repeating the verticals of the two candelabra. In the background a wide opening affords a view of the Mantuan countryside, with the bridge of San Giorgio separating the 'Greater' and 'Lesser' lakes. The figures are vigorously drawn and posed, conveying impressions of plasticity and weight. In combination with the marble pavement and the distant landscape they contribute to the sense of space desired by the artist. The silvery grey light adds a note of both poetry and realism to the scene, an exceptional effect in the painting of the age. The style of architecture and the closely studied landscape are characteristic Renaissance features, though in this picture Mantegna did not introduce the classical ornaments, reliefs and medallions he knew and loved so well.

According to Roberto Longhi this work formed the lower part of a single panel of which the *Christ receiving the Soul of the Virgin* in the Vendeghini Collection at Ferrara was also part. But the supposition presents difficulties both on account of the dimensions and the condition of the paint along its upper edge, proving that the wood was not sawn after completion. It would be necessary to assume that the two portions were separate from the beginning. Berenson considers that the panel here reproduced was painted about 1463, at approximately the same time as those in the Uffizi at Florence. But other critics prefer a date approaching 1492.

Longhi's view would be reinforced if, as Venturi believed, Mantegna, not Andrea del Castagno, was responsible for the cartoon of the mosaic of the *Death of the Virgin* in the Mascoli Chapel of St Mark's, Venice. There is much resemblance in composition between the Prado picture and the mosaic, but in the latter the architecture is richly decorated and the background opening reveals ordinary houses instead of the wonderful landscape which renders the Prado painting so admirable. It was acquired by Philip IV from the effects of Charles I of England. The latter's cipher is branded on the back of the panel.

FRA ANGELICO *Birth and Marriage of the Virgin*

GIOVANNI BELLINI
*Virgin and Child
between two Saints*

BOTTICELLI
*Story of Nastagio*

BOTTICELLI *Story of Nastagio*

BOTTICELLI (SANDRO FILIPEPI), c. 1445–1510
*Story of Nastagio: Retreat and Vision*
Wood: 32⁵/₈ × 54³/₈ in. (83 × 138 cm.) Cat. 2838 (Reproduction p. 110)

Botticelli painted four pictures to celebrate the marriage which united the Bini and Pucci families of Florence. In 1941 three of them were presented to the Prado by Don Francisco Cambo. The fourth belongs to the Watney Collection in London. It is not known exactly whether these paintings were commissioned in 1483 when Gianozzo Pucci married Lucrecia Bini or in 1487 when Pier Francesco di Giovanni Pucci married Lucrecia Bini. In 1568 Vasari described this series as 'pittura molto vaga e bella'.

The four panels, precisely drawn with brilliant, warm colouring, illustrate a tale from Boccaccio's *Decameron;* the one represented here is sub-titled: *Retreat and Vision.*

In this, the first of the series, tree-trunks are used as structural components to separate the different scenes. In the background to the left can be seen the tent among the pines near Ravenna to which Nastagio retired to mourn

his fate in being rejected by the girl he loved. Friends come to visit him from time to time to keep him company in his solitude. In the left foreground he is seen walking despondently in the forest. In the next scene he is astounded by a most extraordinary sight. He prepares to defend a nude woman pursued by a horseman and being attacked by two dogs. In the background the sea with a few ships on it can be seen between the rounded mountains.

As this book was conceived more with the idea of letting works of art be enjoyed rather than for the critical and scholarly study of them, I shall not waste time analysing the observations made by various experts as to the painter of this picture. No-one doubts that it was Botticelli but it has been suggested that possibly Jacopo del Selaio and Bartolommeo di Giovanni, Botticelli's pupil, collaborated with him on the backgrounds of the first two pictures.

110

# SPANISH SCHOOL

## Fifteenth Century

MASTER OF ARGUIS (Anonymous Aragonais), first half of the fifteenth century
*The Legend of St Michael: The Wounded Garganus*. Detail
Wood: $31^{1}/_{2} \times 31^{1}/_{8}$ in. (80 × 79 cm.) Cat. 1332

The remains of this altarpiece are constituted by the predella, two triple-register wings and the top portions of fragmentary panels. They are of very special interest for the study of Spanish painting in the first half

of the fifteenth century. The altarpiece was found in the village of Arguis in the province of Huesca. It already shows, at this early period, features highly characteristic of Spanish art: both what one might call expressionism and also the wish to excite the spectator or at any rate to eliminate dull and flat passages from the pictorial field, as well as unnecessary and otiose items.

The legendary appearances of the archangel Michael inspired miniatures, sculptures and paintings in medieval times. Garganus was said to have shot an arrow at a bull which strayed from the herd. But the shaft rebounded and entered his own eye. The figures of the lord and the herdsman are full of vitality and character, but a certain amount of caricature is evident. The bull is simply and impressively drawn. The contours of the landscape, with its wooded hills surrounding a church intended to represent that of St Michael's Mount, are conventional to the last degree. But these elements remain subordinate to the hagiographical anecdote so pointedly depicted.

The panel representing the *Fall of Antichrist*, after the attempt to scale Heaven, is no less important.

I drew attention some years ago to the very definite traces of humour in these panels, rendering their anonymous author to some extent a forerunner of Bosch.

The altarpiece was placed in the National Archaeological Museum about 1869–71 and transferred to the Prado in 1920.

JAUME HUGUET
*A Prophet*

112

VALENCIAN SCHOOL
*Virgin and Child
with a Knight of Montesa*

BARTOLOMÉ BERMEJO, active 1474–1495 *St Dominic of Silos Enthroned*
Wood: 95¼ × 50¾ in. (242 × 130 cm.) Cat. 1323 (Reproduction p. 114)

We have seen that a superficial understanding of fifteenth-century Spanish painting formerly caused a serious mistake to be made in the attribution of a work by Fernando Gallego on account of its close adherence to Flemish teaching and technique. No such error is possible in the present case. The artist was undoubtedly acquainted with Flemish painting. But his picture is so characteristically Spanish that no hesitation can be felt for a moment. A single detail is enough to prove the point. The lavish use of gold, in particular of gold inlay and relief, can only indicate a Spanish origin.

Such conspicuous features are alone decisive. But we also happen to know how and when the picture came to be painted. It was commissioned by the church of Santo Domingo de Silos at Daroca on 5 September 1474 and finished on 17 September 1477.

The holy Benedictine, seated on his abbot's throne, wears the mitre and a cope embroidered with representations of foliage. He holds a crosier. The figure is imposing and robustly built. Its calm attitude and evident spiritual ardour anticipate, it may be thought, the types subsequently created by Ribalta and Zurbarán.

As in the above-mentioned work by Gallego, the throne is adorned with seven highly naturalistic polychromatic figures symbolizing the three theological and the four cardinal virtues. These decorative sculptural features revive the so-called 'florid' Gothic style.

Bermejo came from Cordova. In the art of his time he occupies a position similar to those of the Catalan Jaume Huguet and the Castilian Pedro Berruguete. Elias Tormo considers him the most vigorous of the primitive Spanish painters.

The work under consideration was presented to the National Archaeological Museum in 1869–70 and transferred to the Prado in 1920.

113

MIGUEL XIMÉNEZ
*Capture of St Catherine*

MIGUEL XIMÉNEZ
*Procession and Apparition of St Michael*

FERNANDO GALLEGO, active 1466–1507
*Christ in Majesty*
Canvas: 66$^{1}$/$_{2}$ × 52 in. (169 × 132 cm.) Cat. 2647 (Reproduction p. 116)

Flemish influence becomes evident in Castile after the middle of the fifteenth century. Prior to that date French miniatures and paintings had set the tone, which was most thoroughly assimilated by Nicolas Francés. Space is lacking for more precise details of Flemish influence at this period; but it should be recalled that in 1429–30 Jan van Eyck had visited Barcelona, Portugal, Granada and Santiago de Compostela.

In 1466–7 a remarkable artist, Fernando Gallego, whose technique is directly related to that of Flanders, was painting at Zamora. Gallego's style is always energetic and impassioned, at times violent. He often painted angular draped figures from memory.

The figure of Christ is enclosed in the fourfold design symbolic of the Evangelists. Two small figures, representing the Church and the Synagogue, are discernible on each side of the Gothic throne.

The types of persons and the colour are unquestionably Gallego's own. But the solemnity of the picture as a whole and its careful execution,

115

coupled with a lack of appreciation of primitive Spanish painting, led to the attribution of this work to Jan van Eyck. It was sent under his name to the Golden Fleece Exhibition at Bruges in 1907, being then the property of M. F. Kleinberger. It was later acquired by the Madrid collector Pablo Bosch, who bequeathed it to the Prado.

FERNANDO GALLEGO, active 1466–1507 *Pietà*
Wood: 47¹/₄ × 44 in. (118 × 110 cm.) Cat. 2998

The dead Christ, taken down from the Cross, lies in the arms of the Virgin. In the background is a Gothic city, almost certainly Jerusalem, between precipitous rocks at whose base a river flows; at the left are the kneeling donors.

The composition and certain details of the panel are a proof of the German and Flemish influences on Spanish painters: the clothes of the donors are reminiscent of Dieric Bouts, the interpretation of this subject was inspired by Rogier van der Weyden and one is reminded of Conrad Witz's colouring.

# FLEMISH SCHOOL

## Fifteenth and Sixteenth Centuries

MASTER OF FLÉMALLE, fifteenth century
*St John the Baptist and Heinrich Werl, and St Barbara*
Wood: 39³/₄ × 18¹/₂ in. (101 × 47 cm.) each. Cat. 1513, 1514

These pictures formed the two wings of a triptych. Nothing is known of the central panel. The backs of the two shutters appear to have been painted: at any rate two halos are discernible on the reverse of that representing St Barbara. But x-ray investigation has not revealed any precise data.

The panels are of capital importance for the study of Flemish Primitives of the first half of the fifteenth century, for they both depict interiors. They are also indispensable for consideration of the work of the mysterious artist given the name of the Master of Flémalle. Not only is their quality exceptional, but they alone, of all the productions available for the elucidation of this painter's personality, are dated. An inscription in Latin hexameters on the lower edge of the panel with St John the Baptist runs: 'In the year 1438 I painted this likeness of Master Heinrich Werl, doctor, of Cologne.'

Some documentary evidence has been preserved relating to the life of Heinrich Werl. He was a Franciscan monk, and in 1441 took part, as a theologian, in the Council of Basle. He wrote commentaries on the Bible and also glosses on the *Sentences* of Peter Lombard. On 1 December 1445 he was at Tournai, perhaps in the capacity of a visiting inspector of the Franciscan Order. He died at Osnabrück in 1461.

The monk is shown kneeling and looking towards the central panel of the triptych, which possibly represented the Crucifixion. A landscape with diminutive figures is visible through the first of the windows. The background wall is furnished with a convex mirror, like that in van Eyck's portrait of the Arnolfini couple in the National Gallery, London, reflecting the side-window and the rest of the room.

St Barbara sits reading, with her back to the fire. She is easy to identify from the tower in course of construction – a regular feature of her icono-

graphy – seen through the window. The perfection of the drawing and the natural appearance of the glass and metal are amazing.

These panels were acquired by the Prince of Asturias, later Charles IV.

Rogier van der Weyden *Pietà*

Rogier van der Weyden
*Virgin and Child*

Style of the Van Eycks
*The Fountain of Living Water*

DIERIC BOUTS
*Adoration
of the Kings*

MASTER OF FLÉMALLE, fifteenth century *Marriage of the Virgin*
Wood: 30¹/₄ × 34⁵/₈ in. (77 × 88 cm.) Cat. 1887 (Reproduction p. 122)

This picture, like others by the Flemish Primitives, represents two different scenes in succession. In the background the High Priest prays at the
altar of the Temple of Jerusalem, while the disappointed suitors of the
Virgin are shown departing; among them St Joseph conceals the flowering
staff, or the rod over which the Dove flies. Different traditions are preserved in the apocryphal Gospels of St James the Greater. The text maintains
that St Joseph overcame certain scruples before deciding upon the marriage.
He considered himself too old and also reflected that he was a widower
with children of his own. The marriage is depicted as taking place in the
open porch of the Temple. This porch, however, is not contiguous with
the main building, the gates of which face a rural landscape.

The numerous episodes are all informed by the characteristic narrative
spirit of Late Gothic painting.

The figures on the reverse, painted in grey tones, are stylistically related
to statues of St James the Greater and St Clara of Assisi. The picture
probably formed one wing of a diptych of which the other would normally
illustrate the Annunciation.

This exceptionally fine work is regarded as one of the earliest by the
anonymous artist called the Master of Flémalle, so-called because
pictures by him, now at the Staedel Institute in Frankfurt, came from a
castle of that name. The painter's reputation is today steadily increasing,
for he is believed to have been older than van Eyck. Jacques Lassaigne

in his *Flemish Painting, the Century of van Eyck*, studies the Master of Flémalle before going on to consider van Eyck himself.

The Prado picture, if compared with those at Frankfurt, disposes of the theory advocated some years ago that the Flémalle master could be identified with the youthful Rogier van der Weyden. The earlier supposition has now returned to favour that he may have been Robert Campin of Tournai, born before 1380 and dying on 26 April 1444.

The vigorous drawing, the merciless realism shown in depicting ugly models and the representation for the first time of silks and women's finery are all typical of the energetic, unsophisticated style, derived from manuscripts and popular tradition, which inaugurated a period of brilliant artistic achievement.

122

ROGIER VAN DER WEYDEN, c. 1400–1464
*Deposition*
Wood: 86⁵/₈ × 103¹/₈ in. (220 × 262 cm.) Cat. 2825

This picture is one of the most important of the Flemish School and in-
disputably the most imposing painted by the artist. The impressively
naturalistic figures look as though they had been carved in stone. They
stand out against a gold background in what recalls a compartment of a

wooden altarpiece and is actually adorned with motives borrowed from the Gothic style of decoration.

The composition of this picture is beautifully balanced by the vertical line of the cross in the centre of the picture and the two groups of three people to the left and right of it and by the two parallel lines of the body of Christ and his Mother. At the feet of St John is a skull which is supposed to be that of Adam, who gave his name to 'Golgotha'. The iconographic details have been expressed with rare perfection – the drawing of the faces and hands and the resplendent purples, blues, greens and reds and the gold brocade robe of Joseph of Arimathea who is supporting Christ's feet. Even more striking is the poignant suffering on the faces of those surrounding the dead Christ and Mary who is fainting.

This picture probably dates from about 1435; it was intended for the chapel of the Fraternity of Crossbowmen at Notre Dame des Victoires, Louvain. Philip II, having given up all hope of buying the picture, commissioned his painter, Michel Coxcie, to make a copy of it. He was satisfied with this copy and on 18 November 1564 ordered the Duke of Alba to pay the artist for his work. This magnificent copy is now at the Escorial. Later Maria of Austria, Queen of Hungary and sister of Charles V, acquired the original. It eventually reached Spain with other pictures inherited by Philip II and was transferred to the Prado in 1939.

The Prado has yet another old copy of this painting. At one time Friedländer thought it dated from the fifteenth century although it is almost certainly early sixteenth-century.

HANS MEMLING
*Virgin and Child
between two Angels*

HANS MEMLING
*Purification*

HIERONYMUS BOSCH *Table-top with the Seven Deadly Sins*

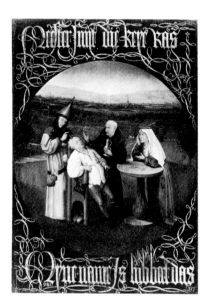

HIERONYMUS BOSCH
*The Cure for Folly*

HIERONYMUS BOSCH
*Adoration of the Kings*

HANS MEMLING, c. 1433–1494 *Adoration of the Kings*
Wood: 37³/₈ × 57¹/₈ in. (95 × 145 cm.) Cat. 1557

This picture is the central panel of a triptych. The wings, which are not
painted on the reverse, represent the *Nativity* and the *Presentation of
Christ in the Temple*.

The scene here takes place in a half-ruined building, with a semi-
circular gallery at the back. The partially demolished walls afford a view
of the road-way, with passers-by. Two of the Kings are kneeling, the
older leaning forward to kiss the feet of the Child. The Negro is entering
the building on the right. The royal attendants stand in the doorways and
a young man, possibly a portrait of the donor, is looking through a

window. The Kings are most splendidly attired. It has been suggested that the two Europeans may be portraits of princes of the Burgundian Court, the elder representing Charles the Bold.

This triptych is more famous than a much smaller one, only 19¹/₄ inches high, belonging to the Hospital of St John at Bruges and dated 1479. It was painted by Memling for Jan Floreins. According to Friedländer the Prado triptych would be of earlier date, about 1470. Its colour organization is more vigorous than that of the work at Bruges.

The magnificent picture at the Prado belonged to Charles V. It formerly adorned the altar of the chapel of the Castle of Ateca, near Aranjuez, whence it was removed to the Prado in 1847.

HIERONYMUS BOSCH, c. 1450–1516 *The Hay-wain.* Triptych.
Centre Panel. Wood: 53¹/₈ × 39³/₈ in. (135 × 100 cm.)
Cat. 2052 (Reproduction p. 128)

When closed, this triptych illustrates the dangers encountered by the traveller on the road of life. When open, the left wing represents the *Garden of Eden,* with the separate episodes of the creation of Eve, her temptation by the Serpent on the Tree of the Knowledge of Good and Evil and the expulsion of Adam and Eve from Eden. The opened right wing shows *Hell* and the centre-piece the *Hay-wain.*

In the sixteenth century Fray José de Sigüenza, an eminent prose-writer and learned historian of the Escorial, quoted Isaiah in explanation of the subject of this work: 'All flesh is grass and all the goodliness thereof is as the flower of the field'. He added a passage from Psalm 102 which may be paraphrased as 'One day in the life of a man is like another. His flourishing is but that of a flower which some wandering breeze barely touches and immediately carries away'. But these references still leave the theme of the picture obscure. The Flemish proverb quoted by H. Wehle throws rather more light on it. 'The world is a haystack and each of us has to make his own way out of it.' Nevertheless, the painter of this most important work must have been inspired by some more definite statement.

On the top of the load of hay on the wain and somewhat overshadowed by a tree a compact group consisting of a man and a woman, three musicians and possibly a pilgrim is flanked by a praying angel and a demon sounding a horn. The wain is escorted by figures on horseback representing

the medieval Estates, e. g. the Pope, the Emperor, a king, a duke and so on. Various other persons try to clamber on to the wain, fall and are crushed beneath the wheels. Heralds announce the advent, through clouds, of the Redeemer. There are six groups along the lower edge of the picture which may or may not represent the Deadly Sins.

The painter's signature appears under the most peculiar of all the groups, that consisting of nuns. The triptych is dated 1485.


HIERONYMUS BOSCH, c. 1450–1516 *The Hay-wain*
Left Wing: *The Garden of Eden*. Right Wing: *Hell*
Wood: 35¹/₈ × 17³/₄ in. (135 × 45 cm.) each. Cat. 2052 (Reproduction p. 130)

The steeply sloping Garden of Eden and its sky represent the setting of the narrative in Genesis, Chapters 1–3. 'The Creator is seen in Heaven, from which the rebellious spirits are falling.' They are shown by the painter as diminutive figures with beating wings subtly and fantastically drawn. Close to a crag of grotesque shape, near the fountain, God the Father is creating Eve. In the centre of the panel Adam and Eve are being tempted by the Serpent, which has a female body and arms. In the foreground of the lower portion of the work Adam and Eve are being expelled from Paradise through a gateway hollowed in the rocks. At the foot of the crag appears the artist's signature. The continued recourse to fanciful ideas, as compared, for example, with the left-hand panel of the painter's *Garden of Delights,* suggests a date prior to 1492. The picture was also certainly painted before Bosch's work was influenced by tales of discoveries in the New World, as the absence of luxuriant flora and fauna proves. According to Felipe de Guevara (d. 1560), author of *Commentaries on Painting* and son of Diego de Guevara, who collected pictures by Bosch in the middle of the sixteenth century, the signature may not have been inscribed by Bosch himself. Guevara makes the remarkable statement that 'one of Bosch's imitators, who had been his pupil, signed his works with the master's name instead of his own, either because he was so devoted to Bosch or because he wished his own productions to be more highly valued'. But in this connection it should be observed that the picture referred to by Guevara is the *Seven Deadly Sins* also at the Prado (Catalogue No. 2822) which is beyond question the work of Bosch himself.

In the right-hand panel, *Hell,* the whole work reaches its climax. The artist several times dealt with the subject, particularly in the *Garden of Delights.* None the less his imagination was never so fertile and terrifying as it is here, in the depiction of the tortures of the damned in Hell or Purgatory. The scene of the right wing here reproduced shows the gateway to Hell as an opening in an unfinished tower, through which naked souls are being escorted either by animals symbolizing the vices which led to their downfall, or else by demons. The flames of Hell are glowing in the background.

HIERONYMUS BOSCH, c. 1450–1516
*The Garden of Delights*
Wood: 86⁵/₈ × 76³/₄ in. (220 × 195 cm.) Cat. 2823 (Reproduction p. 132)

When this large triptych is closed, one of the stages of the Creation, that of plant life, is illustrated in grisaille. The wings are coloured. On the left the Creation of Eve, the Fall and the Expulsion from Paradise take place amid fantastic types of flora and fauna inspired by stories told of the recent discovery of America. The right wing, representing Hell, is conceived with such mysterious power as to be terrifying. It anticipates the Surrealist movement.

The *Garden of Delights* of the central panel, here reproduced, is the name by which the entire triptych is known. The theme is in fact sensuality and the transitory character of sensual pleasures. The chronicler of the Order of St Jerome, who also published a history of the Escorial in 1599, knew this painting as well as he knew the Scriptures. He made a prolonged study of the panel, praising both its execution and its moral teaching. On its delivery at the monastery of San Lorenzo y Real on 8 July 1593, it was described as exhibiting 'the diversity of the world as summarized in various extravagant terms by Hieronymus Bosch'. It was named the *Arbutus* or 'strawberry-tree'. The above-mentioned Hieronymite writes of it as the '*Arbutus* or *Strawberry* panel, symbolizing vain delights and transitory joys'.

According to a study of 1954 by the North American scholar Nicolas Calas the work was inspired by St Augustine's commentaries on the Psalms and those of St Gregory on the Book of Job.

The document which accompanied it to the monastery of the Escorial states that the picture was bought at the auction of a collection owned

131

by Dom Fernando, Prior of the Order of San Juan. A natural son of the great Duke of Alba, he was named Alvarez de Toledo and died in 1591. Like another gentleman of his day, Felipe de Guevara, he was fond of acquiring pictures by Bosch. The surprising taste of certain Spanish noblemen of that time for a style which was already outmoded was shared by Philip II, who somehow reconciled it with his love of Titian's painting.

In 1935 the triptych was taken to the Prado for cleaning and has remained there.

132

QUENTIN MATSYS, c. 1465–1530
*Ecce Homo*
Wood: 63 × 47¼ in. (160 × 120 cm.) Cat. 2801

The unusual angle of vision chosen by the painter to present his scene —
I must apologize for using contemporary terms, but they are precisely
applicable in this case — renders the composition peculiarly striking, an

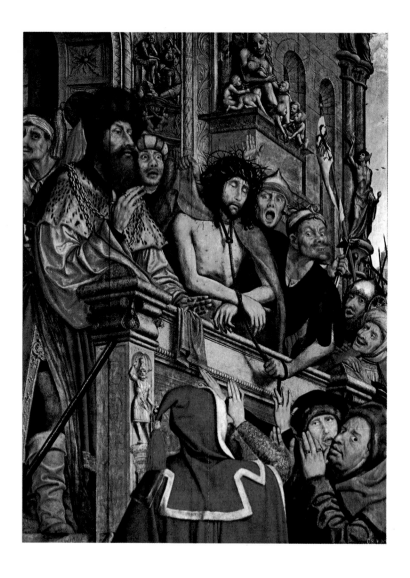

effect which is enhanced by the element of caricature in several of the faces. For Matsys was one of the Flemish artists attracted by the humanism of Erasmus, with its incidental humorous touches.

An engraving by Dürer of about 1498 probably inspired the design.

Friedländer has compared this work with a panel in the Doges' Palace at Venice. But in my view it bears a closer relation to the right wing of the triptych ordered from Flanders by King Manuel of Portugal to provide an altarpiece for the chapter house of St Clare at Coimbra. This altarpiece is now kept at the Machado de Castro Museum in that city. The wing in question shows a certain obliquity of composition, though far less startling than that adopted in the picture under consideration.

The *Ecce Homo* only reached the Prado, in the form of a bequest by Mariano Lanuza, in 1940. Friedländer, however, knew it long before that time and had published a reproduction of it. In his opinion it is a work of exceptional quality, dating from 1515.

JAN MASSYS *The Saviour*

JAN MASSYS *The Virgin*

MABUSE (JAN GOSSAERT), c. 1478–1533/6 *The Virgin of Louvain*
Wood: 17³/₄ × 15³/₈ in. (45 × 39 cm.) Cat. 1536 (Reproduction p. 136)

Architecture in Flanders became very elaborate during the Renaissance. Painters and engravers were much occupied in studying the details of such buildings. Contemporary artists were probably influenced by the structures erected for royal visits to the cities and on other festive occasions. The *Virgin of Louvain* illustrates the style then adopted: an extremely ornate gallery encloses the exedra, or outdoor recess, before which the Virgin is seated with the Child in her arms.

The reverse of the panel bears a long Latin inscription in capital letters stating that in 1588 this painting by Johannes Mabeus was offered by the Louvain municipality to Philip II in gratitude for his assistance during the plague which had ravaged the city ten years before. The picture had been painted some fifty years previously. It would accordingly be surprising if a mistake had been made in the artist's name, especially as several persons were concerned in offering the gift. Nevertheless, Friedländer and other critics maintain that on stylistic grounds the work can only be attributed to Bernard van Orley and that it was executed about 1516. As some hesitation has been felt in discrediting the inscription on the

135

reverse of the panel, the original attribution is still retained, though the objections raised by modern criticism are borne in mind.

The picture was transferred from the Escorial to the Prado on 13 April 1939.

JOACHIM PATINIR, c. 1480–1524 *Charon crossing the Styx*
Wood: 25¹/₄ × 40¹/₂ in. (64 × 103 cm.) Cat. 1616

One of the specialities of the Prado is its collection of late fifteenth- and early sixteenth-century Flemish paintings of a humorous or grotesque tendency. The marked taste of Philip II for the works of Hieronymus Bosch and Patinir is rather surprising. Those of the latter to be seen at Madrid and the Escorial are unquestionably the best by this strange artist.

The picture here reproduced, though less fantastic than the *Temptation of St Anthony,* is a landscape of much originality. A wide stream crosses the scene, joined on the left by a smaller tributary on a different level of the composition. A boat steered by Charon, with a soul as passenger, is passing over the river on its way to the infernal regions of Hades, the gate of which is guarded by Cerberus, the three-headed dog. Buildings and a thicket, from which flames are darting appear on this bank. To the left, on a rock, an angel is visible, while others are half hidden in foliage. A kind of crystal dome can be perceived in the distance. No description or even photograph could do justice to the beauty of the lavish greens and blues of the countryside depicted and the transparency of sky and water.

The combination of fantasy and natural appearances produces a startling effect. In many of Patinir's works the subject is accessory. Occasionally it seems artificially imposed. Other painters, moreover, often collaborated in providing the figures. But in this case the theme is intimately connected with its setting and may even be said to condition it.

The picture, formerly at the Alcazar in Madrid, was salvaged from the fire of 1734.

JOACHIM PATINIR *Rest on the Flight*

PIETER BRUEGHEL THE ELDER, c. 1525–1569 *The Triumph of Death*
Wood: 46¹/₈ × 63³/₄ in. (117 × 162 cm.) Cat. 1393

With Brueghel the vogue of satirical and humorous painting came to an end. He had deliberately adopted an old fashioned style. At his birth, about 1525, Bosch and Patinir were already dead and Quentin Matsys had no more than ten years, at most, to live. But the religious and moral controversies of the day, giving rise to rebellions and wars, still inclined artists to produce works of humanitarian and popular appeal. As we have seen, Philip II and many of the great nobles of his time were particularly appreciative of such painting, though their interest strikes us today as decidedly unconventional for men so immersed in Court ceremonial and dogmatic piety.

As a mocking parallel to the development of Christian doctrine regarding death and the immortality of the soul, the picture here under consideration satirizes society by representing Death as the prospective host of kings, cardinals, feasting guests and lovers. The artist's extravagant figurative imagination precludes any attempt at orderly composition.

Friedländer dates this masterly work at about 1560. His opinion, if correct, would invalidate the argument of E. Michel, suggesting the influence of a work by Brueghel himself, his *Dulle Griet* of 1564.

At the sale of the C. Kreglinger collection at Brussels a picture was included which only differs from the *Triumph of Death* in a few details. It is inscribed with two texts, *Ecce equus pallidus*, from the Apocalypse, 6, 8 and *Ibit homo* from Ecclesiastes 5, which undoubtedly inspired the painting.

*The Triumph of Death* is mentioned in Karel van Mander's book. In 1774 the picture was at La Granja and therefore seems to have been acquired by Philip V.

It was transferred to the Prado in 1827.

PIETER BRUEGHEL *Adoration of the Kings*

# GERMAN SCHOOL

ALBRECHT DÜRER, 1471–1528 *Adam and Eve*
Wood: $82^1/4 \times 31^7/8$ in. and $82^1/4 \times 31^1/2$ in. (209 × 81 cm., 209 × 80 cm.)
Cat. 2178, 2179 (Reproduction p. 142)

Few German pictures are to be seen in Spain, though Flemish painting is very well represented there. The inventories of the royal collections include only a few portraits, hunting scenes and landscapes by German artists. Several of these pictures are attributed to Dürer, but they should be more properly considered as merely belonging to Northern Schools. In the sixteenth and seventeenth centuries many works, not always even German, were current under his name.

Of the four admirable Prado paintings which were signed by Dürer three are of known origin. The fourth, dated 1524, reached the Palace in 1686, though no record of the circumstances is available. The self-portrait of 1498 is dealt with separately. The panels of *Adam* and *Eve*, signed and dated 1507, were presented by Queen Christina of Sweden to Philip IV, who must have been proud to add them to his already splendid collection of works of art. From 1742 to 1827 they were stored, with other nudes, at the St Ferdinand Royal Academy of Fine Art.

These two paintings are the finest nudes produced by the German Renaissance and the most thoroughly classical in style. They are comparable with those of Giorgione and Titian, but lack any suggestion of morbidity

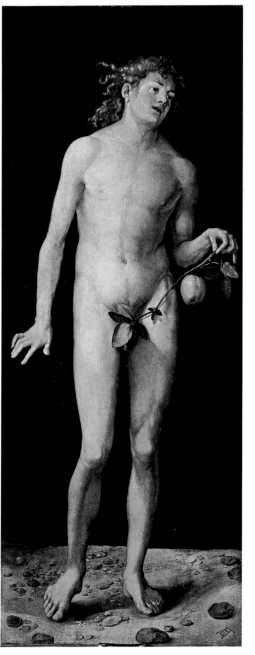

or sensuality. The panels are separate units but could be associated to form a single composition depicting the Fall. The serpent is shown offering the apple to Eve, who has broken off a branch of the tree and given it to Adam. The blast of Satan's breath is so fierce as to impart violent movement to the hair of both man and woman. No background is given to the figures, though stones are scattered at their feet.

There is an early copy of these works at the Uffizi in Florence, containing certain variations, including background landscapes.


ALBRECHT DÜRER, 1471–1528
*Self-portrait*
Wood: 20$^1$/$_2$ × 16$^1$/$_8$ in. (52 × 41 cm.) Cat. 2179 (Reproduction p. 144)

Dürer's exceptional intellectual curiosity renders him the Northern artist closest in genius to the great painters of the Italian Renaissance. There was something in him of both Leonardo and Raphael. Engraver, sculptor, painter and author of treatises on symmetry and perspective, he visited Flanders and spent two separate periods in Italy. But his art remains fundamentally German.

He produced several self-portraits from the age of thirteen onwards. They are dated 1484, 1492, 1493, 1495, 1498, 1500 (?), 1507, 1508 and 1511. Some are pencil drawings, others paintings. Some show him clothed, others nude. Few artists have painted themselves so often.

The Prado portrait is one of his chief works. Dürer was by then mature, aged twenty-seven, and he lavished a great deal of care and skill on its execution. His costume is one of fastidious elegance. His handsome features, framed in long, spiral curls, are set off by a magnificent cap. The hair and beard are most carefully dressed. Yet he does not look like a jeweller's son, but like an aristocrat. The landscape seen through the window is wonderfully well adapted to complete the picture. Green fields bordered by a lake and snow-covered mountains are painted with such topographical accuracy and the light is rendered with such precision as to be comparable with the admirable views produced by Dürer in watercolour, direct from nature, a proceeding rare in his day. The meticulous technique does not detract from the total effect. The feelings of the artist are unerringly conveyed. The colour is brilliant, perhaps slightly garish. In this case the

painterly quality which his works acquired after his visit to Venice is lacking.

A German inscription visible below the window bears the artist's signature and the date 1498.

The picture was presented by the Town Council of Nuremberg to Lord Arundel in 1636 and by him to Charles I. On the latter's death it was bought on behalf of Philip IV. In the reign of Charles II of Spain it was to be found in the Alcazar at Madrid. It is included in the 1828 catalogue of the Prado.

144

HANS BALDUNG GRIEN, 1484–1545
Left Wing: *Harmony or the Three Graces*
Right Wing: *The Stages of Human Life*
Wood: 59½ × 24 in. (151 × 61 cm.) each. Cat. 2219, 2220

Two of the few paintings of the German Renaissance to be found in the
Prado could be placed together to form a diptych. They were executed by

the Rhenish artist Hans Baldung Grien, who died in 1545. He was particularly fond of painting female nudes. But his interest in symbolism and allegory led to a concentration upon detail which renders his treatment of this subject very different from the admirable style of Dürer. In Baldung's nudes a kind of sophisticated morbidity is discernible.

The theme of his composition in the first panel, though the lines are clearly drawn, is not easy to determine. Three young women are represented and three little children, one of whom grasps the neck of a swan, are shown lower down. To the right a viol is visible.

The companion picture no doubt symbolizes the stages of human life.

The reverse of the panel shown on the left carries an inscription which has been damaged by seaming. It originally stated that the picture was presented by Count Frederick de Solms, on 23 January 1547, at Frankfurt-am-Main, to Jean de Ligne, Baron Brabançon, in token of friendship.

The work at one time belonged to Philip II. In 1600 it was at the Alcazar in Madrid and in 1814 at the Royal Palace, whence it was transferred to the Prado. There, until the death of Ferdinand VII, it remained in the room reserved for paintings from the nude.

LUCAS CRANACH THE ELDER *A Hunt in Honour of Charles V at Schloss Torgau*

# ITALIAN SCHOOL

## Renaissance

RAPHAEL
*Visitation*

SCHOOL OF RAPHAEL
*The Holy Family ('La Perla')*

RAPHAEL
*The Madonna of the Fish*

RAPHAEL (RAFFAELLO SANZIO), 1483–1520
*The Holy Family with the Lamb*
Wood: 11³/₈ × 8¹/₄ in. (29 × 21 cm.) Cat. 296 (Reproduction p. 148)

A superb masterpiece of delicate execution, this painting dates from Raphael's Florentine period. It is signed in gold lettering on the edge of the bodice of the Virgin, 'Rafael Urbinus, MDVII'.

The composition and the background landscape, in particular the more distant parts of it, recall works by Leonardo, the figure of St Joseph those of Fra Bartolommeo. But the touching expressions of the Virgin and Child, as well as the refined colour organization, are highly personal features of Raphael's own style.

Lord Lee of Fareham formerly possessed at Richmond a copy comprising a number of variations, especially in the tree on the right. This copy is

147

dated 1504, a year which O. Fischel considers improbable, as he believes that of the original to be in agreement with the evolution of the artist's style. Pedro de Madrazo, in his *Catálogo descriptivo e histórico del Museo del Prado de Madrid* (1872), mentions early copies of this work at Florence, Milan, Pavia and Paris.

Little information is available as to its history. It is only said to have been preserved, on account of its great value, in the 'Treasury' of the Escorial, though there is no ancient authority for this belief. According to José de Madrazo the picture was found there.

It was tranferred from the monastery to Madrid in 1837.

RAPHAEL (RAFFAELLO SANZIO), 1483–1520 *Portrait of a Cardinal*
Wood: 31¹/₈ × 24 in. (79 × 61 cm.) Cat. 299

This half-length portrait, with no particular background, of a sitter whose character and name are equally hard to determine, is one of the most vivid creations of all time produced in this field.

For many the painting represents the most typical of Renaissance cardinals. The peculiarly symbolical character of the portrait is partly due to the mystery surrounding the identity of the model and the number of cardinals' names which have been suggested, sometimes on reasonable enough grounds, in connection with it.

149

The sitter is young, thirty at most, with a bony frame inclined to corpulence, though the features are somewhat emaciated. The profile is aquiline and the eyes are deeply set under carefully smoothed eyebrows. The structure of the lips, especially at the corners, seems to indicate an understanding of, and also possibly a contempt for, emotion.

The economy of means employed by the painter and the penetrating insight with which he has depicted the mentality of his model render this work a most remarkable achievement.

Its exceptional character soon aroused much speculation as to the identity of the cardinal depicted. Of the many names proposed each enjoyed a brief period of general support. They included Dovizzi di Bibbiena, Giulio de' Medici, Silvio Passerini, Antonio Ciocchi del Monte, Luigi d'Aragon and the Swiss Mattia Schinners.

Some years ago W. von Suida pointed out the obvious resemblances between Raphael's sitter in the Prado portrait and one of the group of ecclesiastical dignitaries represented in a picture by Sebastiano del Piombo in the Kress Collection. A handbell on the table in that painting bears the name of Bandellino Sauri. This cardinal had an adventurous career and appears in Raphael's *Disputà*. Sauri was arrested in 1517 and died the following year.

On technical grounds the portrait here under consideration may be attributed approximately to the year 1517. At that period Raphael had reached the height of his powers and was in the habit of employing the help of pupils in his formal compositions, though never in his portraits. That of the cardinal must have been acquired for the royal collection by Charles IV while still Prince of Asturias. In 1818 it was in the Palace at Aranjuez, whence it was transferred to the Prado.

ANDREA DEL SARTO, 1486–1531 *Virgin and Child with Saint and Angel*
Wood: 69⁵/₈ × 53¹/₈ in. (177 × 135 cm.) Cat. 334

This fine pyramidal composition, conforming with the ideas of the Roman Renaissance, illustrates a theme not easy to understand. It does not seem to be concerned with an ordinary Sacra Conversazione, that is, a group of the saints specially venerated by the person who ordered the picture. A definite subject is probably in view, an angel being seated with an open book and the Child leaning towards him as though intending an embrace.

Angels are rarely represented with books. But the explanation in this case may lie in the doubts cast upon the authenticity of the Book of Tobias by a type of criticism rife at the beginning of the sixteenth century and responsible in part for the Reformation. The Book of Tobias relates that the Archangel Raphael accompanied the young Tobias on his journey to the East and that the latter recovered his sight by taking his companion's advice. In del Sarto's picture there is no sign of the fish which played so

151

important a part during the voyage. But it is logical to conclude that the painting proclaims the authenticity of the Book. Such may be the reason why the angel holds a book, while the Child indicates His approval of it by leaning forwards to embrace him.

The other figure presumably represents Tobias. The background shows bare hills and a little village towards which the muffled form of a woman, holding a child by the hand, is walking. But this detail does not seem to have anything to do with the probable theme of the work.

At the Escorial, where Fray Francisco de los Santos, in his 'Description' of 1657, refers to this picture, it was supposed that the figure on the left was that of St John the Evangelist.

The signature may be deciphered on the stool occupied by the Virgin. It consists of two A's, the second of which is inverted, standing for Andrea da Angiolo or d'Agnolo, the artist's surname and Christian name.

This splendid panel, with its brilliant tonality and sparkling colour, was acquired for Philip IV by the ambassador Alonso de Cárdenas at the auction of the effects of Charles I of England after his execution.

In 1819 the picture was placed in the Prado.

CORREGGIO (ANTONIO ALLEGRI), 1494–1534
*Virgin and Child with the Infant St John*
Wood: $18^7/_8 \times 14^5/_8$ in. (48 × 37 cm.) Cat. 112

The great Emilian painter gave a new direction and accent, surprising at the time, to the art of the first half of the sixteenth century. The distinguished critic Bernard Berenson writes, in a somewhat paradoxical phrase, that 'temperamentally Correggio belongs to the French seventeenth century'. The elegant style of this artist, the vivid naturalism of his painting of flesh and his intuitive anticipations of the Baroque manner all suggest that he was ahead of his age. The charming little picture here reproduced is a notable example of the sense of concave form so typical of seventeenth-century art.

The simplicity and tender feeling of the scene, which is built up geometrically in the taste of the day, comes out clearly in the intense light contrasting with the shadows of the grotto and imparting depth to the space dimly visible through the entrance to the cave.

Correggio's refined sensibility, tending to sensuality in some of his other pictures, is evident in the facial expressions of the figures and in the statuesque form of the Virgin, which was probably depicted nude in the first place, as was Raphael's custom.

Selwyn Brinton considers that this work dates from the years 1515–17. The first of the royal collections in which it figured was that assembled by Queen Isabella Farnese at La Granja in 1746.

CORREGGIO
*Noli me tangere*

GIORGIONE (GIORGIO BARBARELLI), c. 1478–1510
*Virgin and Child with St Anthony of Padua and St Roch*
Canvas: 36¼ × 52⅜ in. (92 × 133 cm.) Cat. 288

This picture is a characteristic specimen of the convention of the Sacra Conversazione so much the vogue in Venice. The Madonna is seated on a throne, holding the nude Child upright on her left knee. Judging from the bare leg and customary pilgrim's cloak and staff, the figure on the right is thought to be the Montpellier physician St Roch. The Franciscan

saint on the left is recognizable from the books and lilies on the ground at his feet.

The disposition and balance of the figures recall Giorgione's chief work, the Castelfranco Altarpiece. But the level of execution differs. The Italian picture is the more accomplished, that in the Prado having remained unfinished. Part of the latter's charm is due to the extreme delicacy of the handling of contour, suffusing the whole painting with an atmosphere which enhances the poetic feeling peculiar to Giorgione's style.

The picture was sent to Philip IV by the Duke of Medina de las Torres in about 1650. In 1657, while it was in the sacristy at the Escorial, Fray Francisco de los Santos attributed it, in his 'Brief Description', to 'Bordonon'. This astonishing slip of the pen or rather personal mistake on the part of the monkish author in thus referring to Giorgione led to the absurd ascription of the painting to Il Pordenone. The error is evident from the fact that Fray Francisco states of another picture that it is by 'Bordonon', 'master of the great Titian'. Giorgione's responsibility for the work shown here was re-established by Morelli.

155

It was found impracticable to send this painting to the Exhibition of works by Giorgione and his imitators which was held at Venice in 1955. But it figures in the catalogue prepared by Piero Zampetti, who writes: 'Experts are still divided on the question of attribution as between Giorgione and the young Titian. But in this work the spirit of the Castelfranco master is quite clearly discernible. The seductive charm of Giorgione rather than the dramatic feeling of Titian characterizes it.'

The picture was added to the Prado collection on 13 April 1839.

PALMA VECCHIO *Adoration of the Shepherds*

LORENZO LOTTO *Messer Marsilio and his Bride*

156

TITIAN *Venus with the Organ-player and a Putto*

TITIAN (TIZIANO VECELLIO), 1477?–1576
*Charles V with a Dog*
Canvas: 75⁵/₈ × 43³/₄ in. (192 × 111 cm.) Cat. 409 (Reproduction p. 158)

This picture, painted by Titian at Bologna between 13 December 1532 and 28 February 1533, is the first portrait of Charles V by the artist, who was to become his sole portraitist. The Emperor's passion for the arts – architecture, sculpture, painting and music, and more especially for tapestries and pictures – led him to acquire works of the Early Flemish School (Memling and Bosch) and by the Venetians, which were executed in a very modern technique for the period.

Margaret of Austria, patron of artists and writers, who was the Emperor's aunt and teacher, had a great influence on his artistic formation. To this must be added his inheritance from his maternal grandmother, Isabella the Catholic, and from his ancestors the Dukes of Burgundy. Charles V can be considered as the precursor of royal collections in Spain. His grandfather, the Emperor Maximilian, during the whole of his reign, promoted and protected all artistic enterprises and to this end he gathered together the best artists: Dürer, Cranach, Baldung, Altdorfer and Burgmair. In an engraving of this period, the Emperor is shown in an artist's studio discussing a painting on an easel. Charles V himself says in one of his autobiographical works: 'When a man dies he leaves only his works of art... but money destroys he who uses it to propagate his memory.'

There are many portraits of the Emperor painted by different artists but those by Titian are among the most important as much for the number of

157

them as for their quality. The best of these portraits are preserved at the Prado and among them is the one we have reproduced here. The Emperor is wearing the costume in which he was crowned King of Lombardy. Even though, as already stated, this picture was painted between 1532 and 1533, it did not leave Venice until two years later.

One of the most beautiful portraits of the Emperor painted by Titian is the one where he is represented on horseback at Mühlberg. He is wearing a suit of armour, which is now in the Royal Armoury in Madrid, and a large helmet. He is mounted on a Spanish horse and is galloping towards the Elbe.

Another magnificent picture of the Emperor, seated, was painted at Augsburg in 1548 and is now in the Pinakothek in Munich.

TITIAN (TIZIANO VECELLIO), 1477?–1576 *Danaë and the Shower of Gold*
Canvas: 50³/₄ × 70⁷/₈ in. (129 × 180 cm.) Cat. 425

In a letter of 3 March 1553, Titian offered Philip II three 'poetical compositions'—such was the attractive name he gave to his mythological paintings. One of those referred to in the letter was undoubtedly that reproduced here. The missive reached Philip when he was on the point of leaving for England to contract a second marriage, his prospective bride being a lady of but mediocre charms, Mary Tudor. Philip was twenty-six and had just been installed as King of Naples, so that he could add a royal crown to that of England. The situation was one which contradicts, once more, the legend of Philip's sombre and ascetic character.

The picture is one of the finest nudes in Venetian painting. The colouring is extremely rich, almost sumptuous, the luminosity of the figure of Danaë being enhanced by the play of shadows and the shower of gold in the background.

Philip rewarded the artist with great generosity and obtained from him a promise to complete the painting of *Venus and Adonis*.

TITIAN *Venus with the Organ-player*

A version of the Danaë scene is preserved in the Naples Museum, but it probably preceded the Prado canvas and is in any case inferior. Its composition was criticized by Michelangelo: it is easy to understand that he had little sympathy with an art so far removed from his own aesthetic doctrine.

The Venetian nudes bought and appreciated by the stern Philip II aroused puritanical censure at the end of the eighteenth century, in the reign of Charles III, and were exposed to serious risks. They were rescued by transference to the Academy of Fine Art, where they were kept hidden from the public.

The kings of Spain formerly possessed another *Danaë*, bought in Italy by Velasquez in 1630. It was preserved in the Buen Retiro Palace until Wellington acquired it with the rest of 'King Joseph's luggage', and is now at Apsley House.

160

TITIAN *Venus and Adonis*

TITIAN (TIZIANO VECELLIO), 1477?–1576 *Bacchanal*
Canvas: 68⁷/₈ × 76 in. (175 × 193 cm.) Cat. 418 (Reproduction p. 162)

The landscape represents a seashore, with a ship in the offing. Men and
women are drinking and enjoying themselves in a delightful grove. The
sleeping female nude on the right, it has been supposed, represents Ariadne.
A faun is also lying asleep on a low hill. In the foreground two women
are reading, or perhaps humming the French proverb, 'He who drinks but
once of wine will never know its charms divine'. The right-hand figure
probably portrays Violante, Titian's mistress. There is a prodigal display
in this picture of the most refined and engaging colours. Beauty is incarnate
in the forms of the personages, whose allurements are increased by their
supple attitudes, resembling those of movements in dancing.

161

According to Beroqui the artist was more inspired by certain passages in the works of Catullus than by the *Imagines* of Philostratus, which abounds in descriptions of real and imaginary paintings.

Titian composed his *Bacchanal* as a companion picture for his *Worship of Venus,* also in the Prado, and his *Bacchus and Ariadne* in the National Gallery, London. All three were intended, together with Bellini's *Feast of the Gods* for the palace of Alfonso I of Este at Ferrara.

Philip IV acquired the *Bacchanal* and the *Worship of Venus* on a date prior to 5 August 1658.

TINTORETTO (JACOPO ROBUSTI), 1518?–1594
*Lady revealing her Bosom*
Canvas: 24 × 21⅝ in. (61 × 55 cm.) Cat. 382 (Reproduction p. 164)

The third great Venetian painter of the sixteenth century may be distinguished from his two predecessors — Veronese was actually born ten years later than Tintoretto — by a certain unruliness of temper which led him to produce works of considerable complexity and tumultuous movement, this agitation being one of the hallmarks of his style. But the canvas here in question is exceptional in many ways. It proves that the artist possessed an extremely refined sense of beauty and a greater sensitivity than any other painter of his century to soft and luminous tones of colour. The singularity of this portrait, painted in tints of mauve and pearl-grey, refutes the charge often brought against the classical style of over-emphasizing chiaroscuro and shadow-contrast. For this picture is a splendid example of painting so luminous that it might be thought modern.

There is a certain resemblance between this work and other portraits of women in the Prado. Some experts have therefore believed that it was

TINTORETTO *Susanna and the Elders*

executed by Marietta Tintoretto, the painter's daughter, also an artist, who lived between 1560 and 1590. But in my view the resemblance is one of period and hairdressing fashion only. The close analogy between portraits produced at the same epoch, and indeed between persons of the same century and country, is a matter of common observation. The Marquis of Villa Urrutia, a writer specializing in anecdote and scandal from the beginning of the sixteenth to the end of the nineteenth century, supposed that this fine canvas represented the famous Venetian courtesan Veronica Franco.

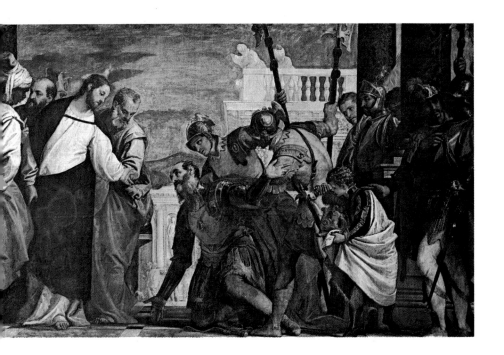

VERONESE (PAOLO CALIARI), 1528?–1588
*Christ and the Centurion*
Canvas: 75⁵/₈ × 116⁷/₈ in. (192 × 297 cm.) Cat. 492

While Titian's work is marked by a feeling for beauty and humanity, the painting of Veronese conveys that love of luxury and wealth typical of the gaiety and nonchalance of Venetian life in his day. Titian's compositions reflect the state of mind of the persons represented. Veronese composed solely with an eye to the development of his scenes and the exploitation of space.

The picture under consideration admirably illustrates this contrast. The subject is taken from the eighth chapter of the Gospel according to St Matthew. All the participants in the scene, richly dressed and armed, stand in a row beneath an archway facing the spectator. The dignity of their attitudes and gestures is well suited to the deeply moving words spoken by the protagonists. In the distance two cloaked ladies, leaning on the balustrade of a terrace overlooking the garden, add a note of mysterious beauty to the action displayed. The young man behind the second of the columns may be a portrait of the patron who commissioned the work, or of his son.

The canvas is unquestionably that mentioned by Ridolfi as in the possession of the Contarini family at Padua. The critic Giuseppe Fiocco considers it a work of the artist's maturity.

D. Angulo points out that the composition somewhat resembles that of the *Lanzas* of Velasquez. But the Court painter of Philip IV could not have known the original by Veronese, which was purchased for the King of Spain by the ambassador Alonso de Cardenas at the London auction of the collection of Charles I. Velasquez, however, may well have seen a copy during his first visit to Italy.

The picture was at the Escorial in 1657. Thence it was transferred to the Prado in 1839.


VERONESE (PAOLO CALIARI), 1528?–1588 *Finding of Moses*
Canvas: 19⁵/₈ × 16⁷/₈ in. (50 × 43 cm.) Cat. 502

The genius of this artist inspired him to the production of vast compositions on canvases of dimensions proportionate to his ambitions. Though the huge and magnificent *Feast in the House of Simon,* at the Louvre, is the largest of all his works, many others are above normal size. Small pictures by Veronese are comparatively rare, but the one here under consideration shows him at his best.

The merits of this painting are not diminished by its modest area. On the contrary the artist has contrived to include within it all his gifts as a colourist and a lover of fine architecture and sumptuous materials.

VERONESE *Youth between Virtue and Vice*

Pharaoh's daughter, her female attendants and Court jester wear the clothes fashionable in sixteenth-century Venice, an anachronism usual at the time. The marble architecture shown is also in the Renaissance style. The treatment of trees and sky adds to the graceful effect of the whole.

According to Hadeln it was painted between 1560 and 1570. Fiocco believes it dates from about 1575.

The work is probably that mentioned by Ridolfi as in the possession of the Marchese de la Torre at Venice.

Veronese often dealt with the subject. Other versions of it by him are preserved in the galleries of the Hermitage, of Lyons and of Dijon.

167

VERONESE *Christ disputing with the Doctors*

VERONESE *Susanna and the Elders*

VERONESE *The Family of Cain wandering*

FEDERICO BAROCCI, 1526–1612
*Nativity*
Canvas: 52³/₄ × 41³/₈ in. (134 × 105 cm.) Cat. 18 (Reproduction p. 170)

The painter has deliberately refrained from showing the more touching features of this traditional scene, in particular its ruined setting open to the chills of December and the nudity of the Child. The Virgin kneels in adoration of her Son, while St Joseph opens the door to the shepherds. The interior depicted is humble but not at all dilapidated. The Child in the crib is well wrapped up against the cold. A basket, bag and bundle are shown on the left and in the centre of the room a kind of knapsack. These inanimate objects are depicted with an attention which it might be an exaggeration to call naturalism but which nevertheless distinguishes this work stylistically from its predecessors.

St Joseph's attitude anticipates the changed conceptions which the Baroque age was soon to introduce. The different levels of the picture are related by a feeling for the third dimension which finds expression, not in a series of varying backgrounds, but by foreshortening of the figures, with a consequent compression of spatial unity. All these details are novel for the period. One might almost call them modern.

Barocci died in 1612, at the age of eighty-six.

This picture was acquired by Charles IV, then Prince of Asturias, a remarkable proof of the unbroken interest in art characteristic of the Spanish kings, even those who were neither particularly cultured nor outstandingly intelligent.

In 1814 this work was at the Royal Palace of Madrid.

# SPANISH SCHOOL

## Sixteenth Century

Juan Vincente Masip, c. 1475 – c. 1550 *Visitation*
Wood: Diam. 23⁵/₈ in. (Diam. 60 cm.) Cat. 851

The study and appreciation of this painter are of recent date, his reputation having been overshadowed by the excessive renown, today on the wane, of his son, Juan de Juanes.

Masip states in his will, dated 1545, that he is elderly. It is accordingly supposed that he was born about 1475. Examination of his works leads to the conclusion that he must have been well acquainted with those of

Raphael and other Italians. It is therefore possible that he may have spent some time in Rome and perhaps also in Umbria.

In his *Visitation* the figures, the landscape setting of the baptism on the banks of the Jordan and the architecture are harmoniously integrated, a proof of the influence of Raphael and the Roman School. But there is here no question of imitation, for the Valencian artist had ideas of his own. He was certainly inspired by a number of the landscapes of Perugino and Raphael. But this view cannot be taken of the woman engaged in spinning, on the left, whose appearance is extremely naturalistic.

Works such as the *St Catherine* by Yáñez and Masip's *Visitation* – to go no further than the limits of the present publication – heralded the imminent maturity of painting of the Renaissance type in Spain, which unfortunately afterwards declined into Raphaelesque Mannerism. Only in its vigorous portraits did this style do justice to the high degree of realism characteristic of Spanish taste.

The *Visitation* was purchased for the Prado by Ferdinand VII, in 1826, from the heirs of the Marquis of Jura-Real.

JUAN VICENTE MASIP *Martyrdom of St Agnes*

LUIS DE MORALES
*The Blessed Juan de Ribera*

LUIS DE MORALES
*Presentation in the Temple*

LUIS DE MORALES, c. 1500–1586 *Virgin and Child*
Wood: 33¹/₈ × 25¹/₄ in. (84 × 64 cm.) Cat. 2656 (Reproduction p. 174)

During a period marked by the widespread influence of frigid Italian Mannerism Spanish piety found in Morales an interpreter it enthusiastically named the 'Divine'. He was born in Estremadura. Very little is known of his life, but it has been asserted that he lived until 1586. He probably spent a long time at Seville, possibly also at Valencia and is, in addition, likely to have visited Portugal. The two Spanish cities were notable artistic centres about the middle of the sixteenth century, and Morales would have had the opportunity to study both Italian and Northern painting there. From these two schools he learnt how to model flesh and render styles of dressing the hair and beard. His deep religious feeling led him to invent touching scenes of obvious popular appeal, depicting the Virgin and Child, where the latter's innocent behaviour foreshadows the Passion. On other occasions Morales took as his subject the *Ecce Homo* story or some passage elsewhere in the Gospels.

His meticulous and deliberately antiquated technique attracted copyists for many years after his death.

The picture here reproduced proves both his 'primitive' tendencies and his acquaintance with the works of Northern painters, derived from

173

Flemish artists working at Seville. Lafuente Ferrari, in his 'Short History of Spanish Painting' published at Madrid in 1946, makes some original observations on the special position occupied by Morales in the evolution of pictorial art in Spain. Certain features of the painter's style remind this author of El Greco, though Morales is not of the same artistic stature.

*Virgin and Child* was bequeathed to the Prado in 1915 by Pablo Bosch.

SÁNCHEZ COELLO
*Mystic Marriage
of St Catherine*

ALONSO SÁNCHEZ COELLO, c. 1531–1588
*The Infanta Isabella, Daughter of Philip II*
Canvas: 45⁵/₈ × 40¹/₈ in. (116 × 102 cm.) Cat. 1137 (Reproduction p. 176)

For both historical and technical reasons this portrait should be compared with that painted by Antonio Moro of his wife Metgen (page 190). It has already been noted that Moro freed himself from the restrictions of Mannerism when he turned from religious painting to portraiture. He was twice in Spain and became Court Painter to Philip II, thus exerting decisive influence on the contemporary school of Court portraiture.

The chief representative of this school was Sánchez Coello, who had been born in the region of Valencia, but was of Portuguese extraction. He had lived with Moro in Flanders and certainly came in contact with him during the latter's residence in Spain. In addition to Moro's example, that of Titian, whose paintings were already on view in the royal palaces, accounts for the sobriety, the elegance and the profound psychological insight expressed in Coello's portraits. But Coello, when he turned to religious themes, became, like his master Moro, a slave to fashionable conventions.

The Infanta has already been mentioned. In 1599 she married her first cousin Albert of Austria, who gave up a cardinal's hat and the arch-bishopric of Toledo to conclude the marriage. As ruler of the Nether-lands she did much for the prosperity of the country and patronized such artists as Rubens and Jan 'Velvet' Brueghel. Isabella had been born in 1566 and was therefore thirteen at the time of Coello's portrait, which is dated 1579. She died in 1633. Her father had been very fond

of her and her nephews Philip III and Philip IV always treated her with the greatest respect.

The painting shows her standing with her hand on the back of a chair, a pose which, together with the plain background, remained characteristic of Court portraits until the time of Velasquez. Coello's elegant handling of clothes and jewellery was maintained by his successors Pantoja de la Cruz and Bartolomé González. In the present case, study of Titian's pictures is evident in the way the velvet of the chair has been rendered.

The work is mentioned in the Prado catalogue of 1828.

EL GRECO (DOMENICOS THEOTOCOPOULOS), 1541?–1614
*Annunciation*
Wood: $9^7/_8 \times 7^1/_2$ in. (26 × 19 cm.) Cat. 827 (Reproduction p. 178)

This work is the only panel painted by El Greco which the Prado possesses. The style is exceptional in showing the influence of his Italian period. I believe the picture was executed about 1577–80, during his first stay of four years at Toledo, though at this early date he rarely gave figures so much importance. A well-known critic, the first to pay serious attention to El Greco, remarked in a striking phrase that in the small painting here in question the artist 'abandoned palaces and porches'. But the recent discovery, in London, of the *Healing of the Blind Man*, a work unquestionably produced in Spain, renders this observation rather less than accurate.

The scene takes place in a porch at the top of a flight of steps which adds an effect of perspective not at first intended by the painter. The figure of the Virgin is given more emphatic and shapely modelling than those which El Greco executed later. That of the Archangel Gabriel is equally conspicuous: the heavenly messenger kneels upon clouds which reflect very little light. Three gracefully designed and grouped cherubs escort the brilliantly illuminated vision of the Holy Ghost.

The workmanship is as detailed as that of a miniature, yet carried out in bold, clear colour. The small dimensions of the picture could never be guessed if one were to see a photograph enlarged so as to render the figures life-size.

The vigour of the composition lends the painting as a whole an effect of serenity hardly disturbed by the extremely submissive gesture of Mary, the 'Servant of the Lord'.

The panel resembles El Greco's larger version of the subject on canvas

at the Barcelona Museum. But the Prado picture does not appear to me to be a later reduction of that work, as is sometimes suggested.

The *Annunciation* here considered was acquired from a private collector on 25 June 1868, while the Prado was still a Royal Museum.

EL GRECO *The Doctor*　　　　　　　　EL GRECO *Don Rodrigo Vázquez*

EL GRECO (DOMENICOS THEOTOCOPOULOS), 1541?–1614
*Portrait of a Gentleman*
Canvas: 18¹/₈ × 16⁷/₈ in. (46 × 43 cm.) Cat. 806 (Reproduction p. 180)

No such objections to the inclusion of the great Cretan artist among Spanish painters can be made as were raised in the case of Juan de Flandes. Yet, as everyone knows, he was already mature on his arrival in Spain in 1577. His undeniable right to be considered a Spanish painter is based on his thirty-seven years of residence at Toledo, during which he continuously painted Toledan personages and landscapes, as well as religious subjects, becoming the faithful interpreter of the Spanish sensibility of his age and influencing the subsequent course of Spanish painting as exemplified in the works of Velasquez, Goya and Solana.

The Prado possesses a unique collection of portraits by El Greco. That here reproduced exhibits all the characteristic marks of the morbid exaltation of the ascetic or mystical type to which the devout leaders of society under Philip II were prone. In this case the whole soul of the sitter has been concentrated by the artist in the eyes. A slight lack of symmetry in the face, together with the shape and slant of the beard, reinforce the feeling of uneasiness provoked by this small canvas, so heavily charged with emotion.

The work is signed in Greek script, 'Domenikos Theotokopolis epoie' and must date from the years 1584–94.

It figured, with other portraits, in the inventories of the Madrid Alcazar drawn up in 1686 and 1700. We may note that the paintings in question had been hung by Velasquez in his studio at the Palace.

The Prado catalogue of 1843 includes this item.

EL GRECO (DOMENICOS THEOTOCOPOULOS), 1541?–1614
*Christ carrying the Cross*
Canvas: 42$^1/_2$ × 30$^3/_4$ in. (108 × 78 cm.) Cat. 822

This subject, together with that of *St Francis in Meditation*, was El Greco's favourite theme. Camon Aznar, in an elegant phrase, suggests that it should be entitled 'The Eyes of Jesus'. Cossio was already aware of seven representations of the scene by El Greco, while Camon, perhaps with some exaggeration, mentions nineteen.

The composition is inspired by the statement in the Scriptures that Christ accepted death for the redemption of humanity.

In view of the simplicity of the design the separate treatments show only very slight variations; consequently, their dating is deduced from technical considerations alone. Their respective merits depend on their different states of preservation and relative cleanliness. Cossio, for example, did not regard the Prado canvas as of much interest, but some years ago, the cleaning and polishing of the varnish revealed the artist's signature inscribed round the lower edge of the Cross and also the high quality of the execution, equal to that of two other versions of the subject by El Greco previously considered superior, that at El Bonillo, Albacete, and the exceptionally fine variant at Huete Hospital.

The features of Jesus closely resemble those of the *Christ Mocked* in Toledo Cathedral, a picture dating from 1577–79. Accordingly, by starting from this date it is possible to establish the approximate order in which the items of the series were produced, the Prado canvas then taking its place at about the period 1594–1604. The hands and eyes especially are prodigiously expressive, and rendered with amazing mastery.

The picture was formerly at the Trinidad Museum in Madrid, to which paintings were conveyed from the convents suppressed during the secularization that took place in the nineteenth century. This particular work was later transferred to the Prado.

EL GRECO
*St John the Evangelist*

EL GRECO
*St Anthony of Padua*

EL GRECO
*St Paul*

EL GRECO
*The Holy Trinity*

EL GRECO
*St Louis of France*

EL GRECO
*Crucifixion*

EL GRECO (DOMENICOS THEOTOCOPOULOS), 1541?–1614
*Adoration of the Shepherds*
Canvas: 39³/₈ × 70⁷/₈ in. (100 × 180 cm.) (Reproduction p. 184)

This work is the most recently acquired and at the same time one of the most remarkable of the pictures by El Greco at the Prado. It was formerly hardly known to admirers of the Cretan artist, for although visible it was difficult to study on account of its position high up on the upper section of the main altarpiece at the Monastery of Santo Domingo el Antiguo in Toledo. Reproductions of it have hitherto been unsatisfactory owing to the dirt which encrusted it, the cracks in the varnish and the dim, lustreless colour.

The colours used by El Greco were of excellent quality and they have not been impaired or become faded, although they are liable to dry out and crumble. It has recently been found that when his paintings are stripped of their varnish or stretched upon new canvas the colours regain their vitality and appear so fresh and brilliant that the authenticity of the works has sometimes been doubted by persons without special knowledge of the artist. This splendid picture was resuscitated in this way.

All its features suggest that it was painted about 1600, at the same time as the works in the Free Hospital at Illescas in the Province of Toledo, while the artist was at the height of his powers. In 1612 the future heirs of El Greco acquired one of the chapels of Santo Domingo el Antiguo as a family vault. The painter's son adorned its altar with the picture in question, which must have been stored in his father's studio for years. During the first third of the nineteenth century the nuns sold two of the panels from the high altar, the *Assumption*, which occupied the centre and is now at Chicago, and the *Trinity*, which was transferred to the Prado. The *Adoration of the Shepherds* was then removed from the chapel, where it had hung for several years, and placed on the upper section of the altarpiece formerly occupied by the *Trinity*.

The canvas was acquired by the State at the end of 1954.

EL GRECO (DOMENICOS THEOTOCOPOULOS), 1541?–1614 *St Sebastian*
Canvas: 46 × 34 in. (115 × 85 cm.) Cat. 3002

The painting of St Sebastian, a naked torso tied to a tree from which the top has been freshly cut off, is among the most beautiful of Greco's works, which rarely attained such perfection.

The way in which the arrows penetrate the body of the stricken martyr is startling indeed. The arrows are, without doubt, as Cossio points out, 'the intoxicating arrows of celestial love'.

Soon after his arrival in Spain, Greco painted St Sebastian for the cathedral of Valencia, where he showed a marked indifference to the classical concept of beauty, which his long stay at Toledo transformed into a spirituality and poignant asceticism.

The forms and the density of the clouds and the translucency of the sky contribute to the profound effect of the painting.

This work dates from the artist's last years: the Prado owns no later work. In the preceding period Greco had painted another very similar version: *St Sebastian,* in the Royal Collection, Bucharest.

The Prado painting was acquired by the Marquis de Casa-Torres who gave it before 1908 to the Marquis de la Vega Inclan. After various transactions it returned to its original owner. It came to the museum in December 1959 as a legacy of the dowager Countess de Mora, mother of the Queen of Belgium, in memory of her father, the Marquis de Casa-Torres, the collector, who was a member of the committee of patrons of the Prado from the committee's foundation in 1912 to his death in 1954.

EL GRECO
*Portrait of a young Knight*

EL GRECO
*St Francis*

EL GRECO
*St John and St Francis*

# DUTCH SCHOOL

## Sixteenth Century

MARINUS VAN REYMERSWAELE, C. 1500–1567
*The Money-changer and his Wife*
Wood: 32⅝ × 38⅛ in. (83 × 97 cm.) Cat. 2567

The subject inspired many artists. According to Georges Marlier, 'pictures representing tax-collectors or money-lenders were popularized by Quentin Matsys and may perhaps first have been painted by Jan van Eyck. The theme has been treated by Marinus van Reymerswaele with the passionate

intensity he displayed in all his actions. Both the elder and the younger Matsys gave such scenes the aspect of a tragi-comedy. In the work of Marinus we find a furious stream of invective being directed against vile swindlers. He produced innumerable replicas and variants of such figures, never more than two, of whom one enters in a book what the other, seated beside him, seems to be dictating, unless he is protesting against what is being written.'

The feeling in the present case is less violent. The work was inspired by Matsys. The Prado possesses two versions, of which one, signed and dated 1538, is now preserved at the Escorial, while the other, executed in the following year, is here reproduced. They vary to some extent in detail.

The later panel was bequeathed to the Prado in 1934 by the Duke of Tarifa.

VAN REYMERSWAELE *Virgin and Child*

LUCAS VAN VALKENBORCH *Landscape with Iron-workings*

ANTONIO MORO
*Portrait of a Woman*

ANTONIO MORO, 1519?–1576 *Metgen, the Painter's Wife*
Wood: 39³/₈ × 31¹/₂ in. (100 × 80 cm.) Cat. 2114 (Reproduction p. 190)

The identification of the sitter is due to V. von Loga, whose arguments are based on the fact that the dimensions of the panel are the same as those of the self-portrait in the possession of Lord Yarborough.

189

The natural pose of the model, the intimacy of the atmosphere and the sobriety of the colouring render this production an admirable work. It forms an ideal companion portrait to that of Mary Tudor, also by Moro, in the Prado collection.

The artist, a native of Utrecht, declined into Mannerism when dealing with religious subjects. But as a portrait painter he laid the foundations of the great school of Spanish Court portraiture which began with his pupil Sánchez Coello and with Pantoja. It culminated in the work of Velasquez, Carreño and Claudio Coello. At the time of the latter's death it had lasted 150 years.

The portrait of Metgen is usually dated about 1554, in the interval between the artist's two visits to Spain.

It was stated in 1666 to be at the Alcazar in Madrid. No other information as to its history is available.

# SPANISH SCHOOL

**Seventeenth Century**

José de Ribera *St John the Baptist*

José de Ribera, 1591?–1652 *Archimedes*
Canvas: 49¹/₄ x 31⁷/₈ in. (125 x 81 cm.) Cat. 1121 (Reproduction p. 192)

Ribera was born at Jativa in the Province of Valencia. But he spent nearly all his life at Naples in the service of the viceroys who governed the city on behalf of Philip IV, for whom he also painted pictures. He always regarded himself as a Spaniard and was even proud of the fact, often adding the words Valencia or Jativa to his signature. These repeated affirmations may perhaps imply that he felt himself to be of the Spanish School as well as Spanish by birth. It has been conjectured that he was trained by Ribalta before leaving for Italy. If so, it was only after undergoing a discipline which would enable him to understand and make technical use of the works of Caravaggio that he came to study that artist. But none of these speculations has yet been proved correct.

Whatever the answers to these problems may be, the fact is that there never was a more *tenebroso* painter than Ribera, one more given, that is, to marked contrasts of light and shade. Yet his development took the direction of a 'luminism' full of novelty.

The most typically Baroque artists, beginning with Rubens, enjoyed depicting the wise men of antiquity. Their style in this field did not lack humour, for their models usually came from the masses of the people. Velasquez, with his paintings of *Menippus* and *Aesop,* achieved outstanding success in this direction. Ribera also cultivated the *genre* and many of his works in this line have been preserved, of which the Prado possesses his *Aesop* and *Archimedes.* The powerful realism of these

191

portraits and the vigour, not to say the fury, of the brushwork undoubtedly impressed certain painters of modern times, such as Zuloaga
and Solana, who both studied the *Archimedes* to their advantage.

The canvas is signed and dated 1630. In the eighteenth century it was
at the Escorial. It appears in the 1843 Prado catalogue.

JOSÉ DE RIBERA, 1591?–1652 *Martyrdom of St Bartholomew*
Canvas: 92¹/₈ × 92¹/₈ in. (234 × 234 cm.) Cat. 1101

Of the five large paintings by Ribera at the Prado, the one here considered
is the richest in colour organization and figuratively the most variegated,
to say nothing of its glowing luminosity.

The composition is eccentric. Two diagonals contrast with verticals
represented by fluted columns and the pole on which the Apostle is being

hoisted. A broad expanse of cloudy sky occupies the upper half of the picture, the lower half being entirely filled with figures. To the left a woman with hard features and an indifferent expression is suckling one of the most attractive infants ever painted. The fascinated observer here has the impression, as is rarely the case, that he is actually witnessing the scene depicted. The imposing nude physique of the martyr proves Ribera's understanding of and feeling for classical art. They prevented him from introducing the grimaces and extravagant gestures to which the development of such a theme so easily gives rise.

The signature on the stone in the bottom right-hand corner reads: 'Jusepe de Ribera español 163?.' The last numeral might be a nought. But Tomo read it as a nine, which seems a more likely figure in view of the evolution of the artist's style.

The picture was deposited at the Alcazar in Madrid during the reign of Philip IV. In 1828 the title is noted in the Prado catalogue.

JOSÉ DE RIBERA *An old Usurer*

JOSÉ DE RIBERA *Jacob's Dream*

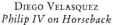

DIEGO VELASQUEZ
*Philip IV on Horseback*

DIEGO VELASQUEZ
*Queen Isabella, Wife of Philip IV*

DIEGO VELASQUEZ, 1599–1660
*Garden of the Villa Medici, Rome*
Canvas: 17³/₈ × 15 in. (44 × 38 cm.) Cat. 1211 (Reproduction p. 196)

During the first visit of Velasquez to Rome, which lasted from 1629 to 1631, he was permitted, by favour of the Spanish Ambassador, to occupy lodgings in the Vatican. When the weather grew very hot he moved to the Villa Medici. But he was obliged to return to the Embassy on being stricken by one of the fevers to which he was subject. He doubtless retained a memory of the delightful gardens at the Villa, with their buildings and statues, for twenty years later, on his return to the Eternal City, he painted two remarkable little views of the Medici gardens.

At that period landscape, with a few exceptions such as Vermeer's *View of Delft* and the *Saragossa* of Velasquez himself, was treated, nearly always in conventional style, as merely the background of a picture. Such effects were contrived in the studio, with no attention to the lighting of nature. But Velasquez in this case had recourse to it. For the first time, he set up his easel in the open air. Veronese, as already mentioned, in his *Venus and Adonis,* had reproduced the patches of light formed by the filtering of sunshine through branches. But he did not repeat this effect, which he had probably noticed by mere chance. Velasquez, on the other hand, observing the same phenomenon, made a careful study of it in the

canvas here under consideration. It is not too much to say that modern landscape painting begins with these two wonderful little works.

The second, here reproduced, was carried furthest. Its interest is heightened by the presence of figures, also treated in 'Impressionist' fashion, and by the tract of country seen through the archway above the statue of Ariadne.

Both paintings illustrate the attention paid by Velasquez to architecture, a taste confirmed by the catalogue of his library, which abounds in the names of architectural treatises.

196

DIEGO VELASQUEZ, 1599–1660 *The Surrender of Breda ('Las Lanzas')*
Canvas: 120⁷/₈ × 144¹/₂ in. (307 × 367 cm.) Cat. 1172

On 15 June 1625 the Dutch General Justin of Nassau surrendered the
city of Breda to the Spanish General Ambrose Spinola, Marqués de los
Balbases.

Velasquez painted this picture for the so-called 'Kings' Room' at the
Buen Retiro Palace in Madrid, prior to 28 April 1635. On the occasion
of his first visit to Italy he and Spinola had both sailed aboard the
same vessel. Consequently, he would then have been able to study the
General's features and undoubtedly learn the details of the surrender.

The composition of this work is the most complex and stately ever
designed by the artist. Its derivation has been traced to an illustration

in a Bible printed at Lyons in 1538, representing the offer of gifts to Abraham by Melchizedek. Attention has been called to the Baroque arrangement of the human figures and horses, forming a sort of St Andrew's Cross on the terrain. But all such technical comments, however shrewd, are forgotten in our contemplation of the realism of the scene, its luminous atmosphere and nobility of feeling. Velasquez had never been to the Low Countries. He could only refer to engravings and paintings, probably of mediocre quality. The fact increases our surprise at his skill in conjecturing and reproducing the character of an environment unknown to him.

He was equally successful in his renderings of typical Dutch soldiers and their behaviour, though he could have had little opportunity of encountering them at Madrid.

Yet over and above all such pictorial triumphs the most striking impression conveyed is that of the moral grandeur of the protagonists. The conqueror receives his vanquished enemy with a magnanimity to which, if the story is true, only so magnanimous and deeply sensitive an artist as Velasquez could hope to do justice.

So far as the origin of the composition of the central group is concerned, it may perhaps be referred to a print by Pieter de Iode (1606–1674) entitled in Latin 'Reception of the Cardinal Infante of Cologne, whose presence exceeds all expectation, by the Electoral Princes'. But I have been unable to discover the date of this engraving.

DIEGO VELASQUEZ
*The Spinners ('Las Hilanderas')*

D<small>IEGO</small> V<small>ELASQUEZ</small>, 1599–1660 *The Topers (The Triumph of Bacchus)*
Canvas: 65 × 88⅝ in. (165 × 225 cm.) Cat. 1170

The subject is treated in accordance with the current conventions of mythological painting in contemporary Italy, Flanders and France, but also in the burlesque style typical of Spanish literature and art. Further examples are to be found in the *Forge of Vulcan and Mars.*

The contrast between the naked god crowning a soldier victorious in a drinking competition and the poverty-stricken, shabbily dressed spectators of the scene is repeated in that between the finely wrought goblets of

Venetian glass and the coarse earthenware of the white cup and common wine-jar.

It is highly probable that Velasquez was inspired by an older picture, for he habitually worked in this way. A description exists of festivities at Brussels in the year 1612, held in the presence of Isabella Clara Eugenia, which included a procession oddly suggestive of the work here considered. 'The god Bacchus, nude, is seated astride a wine-barrel ... two bunches of grapes adorn his ears ... he is accompanied by eight young men who are paying him homage.'

The still-life components of the canvas are subordinated to the compact composition and the uniform light which falls on all the figures except that in the left foreground, so disposed as to reinforce the effect of recession.

The picture has been called 'a frozen bacchanal'. It would be more accurate to compare it with a snapshot.

The work was purchased from the painter himself on 22 July 1629, just before his first visit to Italy. The fact suggests that it was painted during the second, prolonged residence of Rubens at the Spanish Court, when the two artists became friends.

The canvas has been preserved without any attempt at relining.

DIEGO VELASQUEZ
*The Court Jester
Don Diego de Acedo
('El Primo')*

DIEGO VELASQUEZ, 1599–1660
*The Maids of Honour.* Detail
Canvas: 125¹/₄ × 108⁵/₈ in. (318 × 276 cm.) Cat. 1174 (Reproduction p. 202)


The scene here illustrated seems to have come about in the following way. One summer day in 1656 Velasquez was painting portraits of Philip IV and Queen Mariana at the Alcazar in Madrid, occupying the 'Prince's Room', an apartment below ground level which was adorned with copies by Mazo of pictures by Rubens and Jordaens. The little princess Margarita, aged four, accompanied by her most trusted attendants, was present at the sitting. With her were two young noblewomen, known in the royal household as *meninas,* meaning 'girls' in Portuguese, the Court Jester, Nicolasito, the female dwarf Maribárbola, a duenna whose name is not known and Doña Marcela de Ulloa. At the feet of this group lay a dignified, noble-looking mastiff. The child being thirsty, one of the *meninas* presented her, as the custom was, with a vessel containing cold, perfumed water. At that moment José Nieto Velasquez, the chamberlain, unexpectedly entered through a door at the back of the room, bringing a flood of sunlight in with him. The painter had his back to all these people, but noticed the plastic interest of their grouping and the beauty of its colour. In order to study it he took up a position beside his royal models, whom he then ceased painting, and began the new subject, keeping the participants in the scene just where they stood, exactly as if some other painter were about to set down this momentary, domestic incident of palace life, immortalize the instant and record it for ever in the aesthetic sensibility of mankind.

No doubt the subject is no more than such an interior as Flemish and Dutch artists have made familiar. But the genius of Velasquez was then at its height. In this canvas he has solved the problem of representing aerial perspective and environment through colour, succeeding so perfectly that if the picture is studied with deliberation and in solitude the spectator becomes absolutely convinced that the painted space is real, that the figures live and are about to move. The past comes to life again.

Velasquez may well have been thinking, in a technical sense, of the many interiors with a mirror in the background painted by such artists as van Eyck and the Master of Flémalle. But in this case he used the

201

device to lead the eye across the spatial interval between the mirror and the foreground group, thus giving the observer an almost physical sensation of the area covered by the picture.

Diego Velasquez *Philip IV*   Diego Velasquez *The Infante Don Carlos*

Diego Velasquez, 1599–1660
*The Infanta Margarita of Austria, afterwards Empress*
Canvas: 81¹/₂ × 57⁷/₈ in. (221 × 147 cm.) Cat. 1192 (Reproduction p. 204)

In this portrait the central figure of the *Maids of Honour* has reached
the age of eight or nine. She was born to Philip IV and his second wife,
Mariana of Austria, on 12 July 1651. At the age of sixteen she married
the Emperor Leopold. She died on 12 March 1673.

Velasquez painted several portraits of her. Of the first, a standing full-
length, one version is in the palace of the Dukes of Alba at Madrid,
and another, more detailed, in the Vienna Museum. A later half-length
is in the Louvre. A further portrait, probably to be dated 1657 and in
the Vienna Museum, shows her dressed in white. In still another, she
wears greyish-green. The last of the series and perhaps the last of all
the artist's paintings, is the portrait here reproduced.

203

It is doubtful whether the neck and the hands were the work of Velasquez. But the extraordinarily skilful handling of the face and dress is
unquestionably his. The luminous, transparent handkerchief, the diamonds
and the wonderfully subdued tints of the skirt are amazing.

The picture at the Vienna Museum called the *Family of Mazo*—who
was the son-in-law of Velasquez and himself a painter—represents a studio
where Velasquez is painting a portrait. It seems to be the same as that
here reproduced, but cannot be, for the Infanta wears blue, not pink.

204

FRANCISCO ZURBARÁN, 1598–1664 *St Casilda*
Canvas: 72½ × 35⅜ in. (184 × 90 cm.) Cat. 1239

This painting could reasonably be considered the portrait of an Andalusian lady, subsequently mistaken for the saint on account of the roses in her lap. For the legend states that Casilda, daughter of a Moorish king, distributed pieces of bread, which turned to roses, among the Christian captives of her father.

Religious pictures of this kind, in all probability drawn from the life, were common. Two seventeenth-century Spanish poets, Ulloa Pereira and Esquilache, wrote verses entitled respectively: 'In Praise of a Lady acting as a Model for St Lucy' and 'To a Lady painted with the Attributes and Robes of St Helena'. These quaint poems, discovered by the learned

critic Emilio Orozco, explain what might otherwise appear an astonishing practice in the art of a nation so devout and so strict in its observances as Spain. Zurbarán of course painted a great many female saints in seventeenth-century dress and these figures were copied by his pupils. But only a few such works can be regarded as portraits.

The elegance of the sitter's attitude and of her costume of thick and heavy silk, the folds of which were doubtless studied on a lay figure, together with the warm, glowing colour scheme, render this picture a perfect example of the style of the Spanish painter most admired today. His command of the expression of volume and the apparent hardness of his surfaces, combined with his patience and resolution in the representation of physical quality and finally his disciplined sensibility, never affected or superficial, exercise an exceptional degree of fascination upon modern artists and connoisseurs.

The picture does not figure in the inventories of the Royal Palace of Madrid before 1814. In 1828 it is included in the Prado catalogue.

FRANCISCO ZURBARÁN
*St Peter Nolasco's Vision
of St Peter the Apostle*

FRANCISCO ZURBARÁN
*Still-life with four Vessels*

BARTOLOMÉ ESTEBAN MURILLO
*The Children with the Shell*

BARTOLOMÉ ESTEBAN MURILLO
*A Galician Girl with a Coin*

BARTOLOMÉ ESTEBAN MURILLO, c. 1618–1682 *The Immaculate Conception*
Canvas: $105^7/_8 \times 74^3/_4$ in. (274 × 190 cm.) Cat. 2809 (Reproduction p. 208)

The Virgin, standing on a crescent moon, is surrounded by angels and clouds which accentuate the diagonal design to the right.

Very handsome models were used for the figures of the Virgin Mary and the angels. The expression of the former suggests both divinity and humanity. The many subtly graded tones are mainly golden, though dulled in places by the remains of old varnish, which should be removed.

The attractive colouring of Murillo's works accounts for his continued popularity among the general public. But art historians and modern painters consider his chromatic effects over-facile and meretricious. They are inclined to deprecate him for this reason. It is certain, however, that closer examination of his numerous productions would restore Murillo to the rank at present denied him.

The subject of the canvas here considered has been misunderstood. It has been erroneously regarded as an Assumption, though it is in fact a statement of the privilege accorded by God to the woman He chose to be the mother of the Saviour, in preserving her, from the first instant of conception, from the stain of original sin transmitted by Adam to all his descendants. The theme is not really susceptible of expression in plastic terms. But it inspired both painters and sculptors in Spain to illustration by the conventional device of the portrait of a child or girl 'in glory'. The cult of the Virgin Mary struck deep roots in the country and reached a climax at Seville in the seventeenth century.

Murillo exceeded all other artists in the quantity and quality of his treatments of the subject, of which the Prado possesses three other very fine examples. That here reproduced, painted about 1678 for the Hospital de los Venerables at Seville, surpasses them all in majesty and serene beauty.

It was removed to France by Marshal Soult in 1813. At his death it was acquired by the Louvre for 615,000 francs. In 1940 it was exchanged, by agreement with the French Government, for the first portrait by Velasquez of Queen Mariana, now in the Louvre.

# FLEMISH SCHOOL

## Seventeenth Century

Sir Peter Paul Rubens, 1577–1640
*Diana and her Nymphs surprised by Satyrs*
Canvas: 50³/₈ × 123⁵/₈ in. (128 × 314 cm.) Cat. 1665

The scene is a forest where Diana and her nymphs have been hunting.
To the left a fox and a stag are to be seen and to the right a boar. The
huntresses had been quietly resting when four satyrs unexpectedly appeared
and tried to seize four of the nymphs by force. The goddess is shown
about to hurl her spear at the insolent intruders, who are also being
attacked by dogs.

The sinuous line of the composition and the frieze-like disposition of
the figures furnish an example of the dominant emphasis on rhythm
sometimes to be observed in painting, when a fictitious musical character
is given to both design and colour, just as in the art of ballet, where
drawing, modelling, colour and sound are combined. The canvas illustrates,
by its organization of pleasing tones, the gifts of Rubens as a colourist.

It was fashionable at the end of the last century to exaggerate the
contributions of Rubens' pupils to his work. Accordingly, the background

and the animals in the painting here considered were then attributed by some critics to Jan Wildens. But the present tendency is to restore almost the entire production of this great man's studio to his own hand.

This work was executed in his last years, between 1636 and 1640.

SIR PETER PAUL RUBENS
*Nymphs and Satyrs*

SIR PETER PAUL RUBENS, 1577–1640 *The Triumph of the Church*
Wood: 33⁷/₈ × 35⁷/₈ in. (86 × 91 cm.) Cat. 1698

Rubens was endowed with a prodigious facility of invention. His exuberant imagination was given full scope by the command of his sovereign, the Infanta Archduchess Isabella, ruler of the Low Countries, to execute a number of cartoons, seventeen according to the most precise calculations, for a series of tapestries, illustrating the institution of the Eucharist. The tapestries were destined for the convent of the Royal Barefoot Sisterhood in Madrid. By 1628 Rubens had completed his designs on panels. The so-called 'cartoons', though really on wood, were finished in his studio before being entrusted to Jan Raes and Jacob Geubel for weaving.

The symbolism in this case is obvious. The figure seated on the chariot, carrying the Holy Sacrament, represents the Church. The reins are held and the horses led by the Cardinal Virtues. Fury, Discord and Hatred writhe beneath the wheels. The figures on foot, apparently yoked to the

car, are Blindness and Ignorance. The foreground shows the Globe, encircled by Evil in the form of a serpent biting its tail.

The greatest care was evidently taken, despite the artist's characteristic bold style, in delineating the forms. They are not really sketches.

The Prado series of panels formerly belonged to Luis Méndez de Haro and later to his son, Marquis of Eliche and Viceroy of Naples. At the auction which followed the latter's death the panels were acquired by Charles II of Spain. They are listed in the royal inventory of 1694. Items were then to be found at the Prado, the Retiro and the Royal Palace. Eight were eventually retained by the Prado, which also had a copy of a ninth item. Since July 1956 the entire series has been placed in one room. Only one other design for the series is known, *Elijah and the Angel* at Pau.

SIR PETER PAUL RUBENS
*St George and the Dragon*

SIR PETER PAUL RUBENS
*The Three Graces*

SIR PETER PAUL RUBENS *The Garden of Love*

SIR PETER PAUL RUBENS *The Judgment of Paris*

FRANS SNYDERS, 1579–1657 *Fox and Cat*
Canvas: $71^1/_4 \times 40^1/_2$ in. (181 × 103 cm.) Cat. 1755 (Reproduction p. 214)

The works of Snyders are among the most important assets of the Prado collection, constituting a different category of painting from those of his compatriots. Some twenty canvases of excellent quality make a visit to the Prado imperative for those interested in this great animal painter, both with respect to his hunting scenes and his illustrations of Aesop's fables. He also painted groups of birds, studies of still-life and portraits.

Attempts have been made recently to attach more value to the pictures by this artist than they deserve, decrying those of Rubens by comparison. But such extravagant estimates have not been generally accepted.

The work here reproduced, owing to the variety of animals depicted in it, the vigour of its execution and its highly skilled composition, enables a good idea to be formed of the painter's talents.

A tree, as usual, dictates the disposition of the animals shown. On the ground a fox which has caught a hare replies with yelps to the mewing of an enraged cat which has climbed the tree. Two squirrels and two stoats scamper among the branches. A monkey looks on. In the right-hand bottom corner five kittens are playing, while another approaches the group of the fox and hare.

213

The accurate rendering of the animals' forms and attitudes, and of their fur, coupled with the dexterous composition and the luminosity of the background landscape, gives the painting, which is signed by the artist, high decorative value.

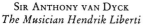

SIR ANTHONY VAN DYCK
*The Musician Hendrik Liberti*

SIR ANTHONY VAN DYCK
*The Painter Martin Ryckaert*

SIR ANTHONY VAN DYCK, 1599–1641 *Sir Endymion Porter and the Painter*
Canvas: 46$^7$/$_8$ × 56$^3$/$_4$ in. (119 × 144 cm.) Cat. 1489 (Reproduction p. 216)

Van Dyck was able to satisfy his aspirations to elegance and good taste
by mingling with the fashionable world. He became the intimate friend
of an English magnate, Sir Endymion Porter, born at Madrid and secretary
for Spanish affairs to the Duke of Buckingham. In 1622 Porter had been
sent by the Duke to the Court of Philip IV to discuss the projected
marriage of Charles, Prince of Wales, to Maria, sister of the Spanish King.
Sir Endymion also happened to be a connoisseur and collector of works of
art. He died in 1649. Van Dyck must have been proud to portray so
eminent a personage.

Elegance, though of a kind distinct from that of Velasquez, characterizes
every feature of this double portrait, from the arrangement, attitudes and
clothing of the figures to the background landscape, the curtain and the
column. These accessories were all to be repeated in the Court portraits
of the ensuing period.

Van Dyck was actually the initiator of the English School of portraiture.
The fact appears more clearly in this picture than in any other.

The canvas was painted about 1623. It was acquired by Isabella Farnese,
the second wife of Philip V, and figures in the La Granja inventory of 1746.

Jacob Jordaens, 1593–1678
*Three Itinerant Musicians*
Wood: 19¹/₄ × 25¹/₄ in. (49 × 64 cm.) Cat. 1550

The position of Jordaens, as a contemporary of Rubens and van Dyck, made it almost impossible for him to develop an individual style. Some hesitation is therefore felt about the authenticity of certain works attributed to him, for example the *Mystical Marriage of St Catherine*, at the Prado, which a number of specialists in Flemish painting believe to be van Dyck's. But in other cases there seems, to me at any rate, no room for doubt.

216

Max Rooses thinks that Jordaens may not have painted the *Itinerant Musicians*, for the models used there do not appear in his other pictures. Hysmans suspects the hand of van Dyck. But close study must lead to a rejection of this hypothesis, for nothing could be further, technically, from the familiar methods of the great portraitist. The breadth and vigour of the strokes by which the figures are built up never characterize the works of van Dyck. Nor do they bear any relation to the style of Rubens even in the latter's sketches. The execution of this painting and in particular

the handling of the figures remind one of the early Impressionist experiments. It is not surprising that the panel was reproduced in a book on nineteenth-century tendencies in painting and described as a curious and isolated precedent of the later movement. The realism with which the three young men have been treated is as exceptional in the work of Jordaens as is the realism applied by Rubens to the portrait of Marie de' Medici compared with the rest of the artist's production. Both pictures, therefore, deserve special attention.

There is no trace of the *Itinerant Musicians* in the royal inventories. It is only known that the panel reached the Prado in 1827.

JACOB JORDAENS
*The Artist's Family in a Garden*

JACOB JORDAENS
*Goddess and Nymphs after Bathing*

# DUTCH SCHOOL

## Seventeenth Century

WILLEM CLAESZ HEDA *Still-life*

GERRIT VAN HONTHORST, 1590–1656
*Incredulity of St Thomas*
Canvas: 49¼ × 39 in. (125 × 99 cm.) Cat. 2094 (Reproduction p. 220)

Reference has been made above to the reasons why so few examples of the Dutch School are to be found in the royal collections of Spain.

This picture illustrates the scepticism with which the Apostle Thomas, who had been absent during the various events that followed the Crucifixion, heard the news of the Resurrection. The artist has indicated his incredulity with dramatic violence, heightened by the sombre colours employed. Honthorst lived for some time in Italy, where he became famous, and at that period deep shadows were the fashion among painters. The canvas here considered is an excellent example of this important

development in the history of art, parallel with the advent of realism and the elevation of effects of light to a leading feature of the work as a whole.

A. von Schneider, the historian of Dutch art, in a book published in 1933, denies that Honthorst painted this picture. He attributes it to Mathäus Stomer, Honthorst's pupil in Rome.

The work was salvaged from the fire of 1734 and in 1772 was at the Royal Palace in Madrid.

REMBRANDT, HARMENSZ VAN RIJN, 1606–1669 *Artemisia*
Canvas: 55$^7$/$_8$ × 60$^1$/$_4$ in. (142 × 153 cm.) Cat. 2132

Doubts have been felt as to the meaning of this picture. But the traditional explanation seems reasonable. The Pergamene queen is richly dressed, her attitude majestic and she is being presented with a jewelled offering in the form of a shellfish, the nautilus, by a slave-girl. In the background a masterly handling of chiaroscuro reveals the figure of an old woman.

The model for Artemisia may have been Saskia van Uylenborch, whom Rembrandt married in 1634, the very year in which he signed the picture with a somewhat ostentatious flourish. The conclusion has been drawn that the work represents a pledge of conjugal fidelity. Schmidt-Degener, Director of the Rijksmuseum, Amsterdam, stated however that the features of the model for Artemisia were not those of the painter's wife. But whether such details are felt today to add to the interest of this painting or detract from it, they can make no difference to its evident merit. Schmidt-Degener, an expert on Rembrandt's work, considered the *Artemisia* the most important picture of its year.

It may be observed that the two portraits of Saskia, in the Cassel and Dresden Galleries, which are not dated but presumed to be of 1634, give her a more youthful aspect, suitable to her age of twenty-two, than that of the *Artemisia*.

The canvas was one of twenty-nine selected by Charles III in 1769 at the sale of the collection of the Marques de la Ensenada, one of the best ministers who served under Ferdinand VI.

It was at the Palace in 1772.

JACOB VAN RUISDAEL *A Wood*

NICOLAS POUSSIN, 1594–1665
*Landscape*
Canvas: $47^1/_4 \times 73^5/_8$ in. ($120 \times 187$ cm.) Cat. 2310

The countryside round Rome made a profound impression on Poussin and he spent many years there. His relevant landscapes, based on memory and fragmentary notes taken at the time, do not pretend to material accuracy. He worked up his basic data by subsequent reflection, discarding their immediate, superficial effect on him. The landscapes including monuments were also 'revised' later in almost every case. They are saturated with

melancholy feeling. The figures that give them 'animation'—if the word is not too strong here—might just as well be replaced by statues or the statues by figures. These works conveyed a deep sense of ancient poetry and formal beauty. But they could not be expected to have any popular appeal.

The Prado collection of Poussin landscapes, amounting to five, is exceptional both in quantity and quality. The dominant tone of the one reproduced is a yellowish grey, reinforced by contrasting blues, and the canvas dates from about 1650.

NICOLAS POUSSIN *Parnassus*                    NICOLAS POUSSIN *Bacchanal*

CLAUDE LORRAIN, 1600–1682 *Embarkation of St Paula at Ostia*
Canvas: 83¹/₈ × 56³/₄ in. (211 × 145 cm.) Cat. 2254

This work was ordered from Claude by Philip IV as part of an extremely important undertaking. A series of four canvases was commissioned, of which two were to be on Biblical subjects, the *Finding of Moses* and *Tobias and the Archangel Raphael*, while two had to illustrate episodes from Roman hagiographical sources, the *Burial of St Serapia* and the *Embarkation of St Paula at Ostia*.

The classical construction, the figures and the extraordinary luminosity of the *Embarkation* render it the chief of these productions. From the foreground, where the Saint and her attendants are descending the steps, right on to the furthest distance, where the light is hard, almost grating,

the eye has the impression of an unbroken journey into space. This third
dimension is not obtained, as in other landscapes, by a series of successive,
separate planes like those of stage scenery, but by light which envelops

the painting as a whole and, in a word, unifies it. The composition of the imaginary region depicted is a perfect miracle of skill.

Claude himself was certainly responsible for the linking up of the figures with the various compositional elements, though it is often asserted that Filippo Lauri or Jacques Courtois may have contributed to the picture.

An Italian inscription reads: 'Embarkation of St Paula the Roman for the Holy Land.' On the back there is: 'Portus Ostiensis A et Tra.'

In the eighteenth century the picture is recorded as being at Buen Retiro. In 1828 it appears in the Prado catalogue.

CLAUDE LORRAIN *A Hermit in a Landscape*

CLAUDE LORRAIN *Temptation of St Anthony*

JEAN-ANTOINE WATTEAU, 1684–1721 *Festivity in a Park*
Canvas: 18⁷/₈ × 22 in. (48 × 56 cm.) Cat. 2354

This delightful artist added to the representations of popular merrymaking which had been produced by Flemish painters throughout the seventeenth century a refined, poetic feeling which differentiates his work from all previous achievements in this field. It was he who endowed eighteenth-century art with its most appreciated features. An often morbid sensibility is always evident.

227

The two charming little pictures at the Prado were already attributed to Watteau a few years after his death, in the collection of Isabella Farnese at La Granja de San Ildefonso. According to M. J. Methey, drawings for some of the groups of figures were also preserved. There can be no justification, therefore, for the recent ascription of the paintings to Quilliard, of all people.

Everything in the work here reproduced contributes to the general impression of tender sentiment, from the dark, wooded setting with its marble fountains adorned with statues of Ceres and Neptune to the young couples in their graceful, elegant costumes and the subtle glow of delicate colour.

This painting was at the Aranjuez Palace in 1794 and at that of Madrid in 1814, whence it was transferred to the Prado, where it figures in the catalogue of 1828.

JEAN-ANTOINE WATTEAU *The Marriage Contract*

# ITALIAN SCHOOL

## Seventeenth and Eighteenth Centuries

Guercino *Susanna and the Elders*

Francesco Furini, c. 1600–1646 *Lot and his Daughters*
Canvas: 48³/₈ × 47¹/₄ in. (123 × 120 cm.) Cat. 144 (Reproduction p. 230)

In this case the artist was inspired by the improprieties of the story in Chapter 19 of the Book of Genesis to paint one of his best pictures. It certainly has a more sensual character than any other in the Prado collection which, though rich in nudes by, for example, Titian and Rubens, possesses very few specimens of licentious art.

The successive episodes of the Biblical text are here combined in a single scene. Furini was thus able to achieve a high degree of plasticity, effected by a colour scheme in which a most admirable deep blue predominates. The peculiar contrast of this blue with the green of the draperies half covering the figure on the right is also very striking.

Though he died as early as 1646, certain aspects of his style anticipate some of those to be noted in French artists of the eighteenth century.

In 1701 this picture was at the Buen Retiro Palace. In 1792 it was transferred, with other nudes, to the Royal Academy of Fine Art. Thence in 1827, it passed to the room at the Prado reserved for paintings from the nude.

Giovanni Battista Tiepolo, 1696–1770 *Olympus*
Canvas: 33⁷/₈ × 24³/₈ in. (86 × 62 cm.) Cat. 365

The last of the great Venetian painters reached Madrid on 4 June 1762 and died there in 1770. He had been summoned to decorate the ceilings of the Throne and Guard Rooms of the new Royal Palace. After carrying

GIOVANNI BATTISTA TIEPOLO *Abraham and the three Angels*

out this work he remained in Madrid, devoting himself to religious pictures. But it is probable that he sketched a few designs for frescoes to adorn the large number of still undecorated ceilings at the Palace.

The luminous *Olympus* canvas, like others of its kind, was doubtless painted in anticipation of a commission.

Strictly speaking, there is no subject. The theme is unrestricted and owes something to the artist's imagination. The figures of gods and goddesses, among whom it is possible to recognize Saturn, Minerva, Venus, Diana, Juno, Jupiter and Mercury, are grouped in a spiral composition of the type much cultivated by Tiepolo. The sky and clouds are treated as substantial components of the total effect. The colour is as gay and delicate in tone as in any of the best frescoes of the artist.

This work had already reached the Prado by 1834. The inference is that it had come from the Royal Palace, where it may well have been part of the preparation for a ceiling decoration.

232

# SPANISH SCHOOL

## Eighteenth Century

MELÉNDEZ *Still-life*

LUIS EUGENIO MELÉNDEZ, 1716–1780
*Still-life with Salmon, Lemon and Three Vessels*
Canvas: 16¹/₂ × 24³/₈ in. (42 × 62 cm.) Cat. 902 (Reproduction p. 234)

It is a commonplace of criticism, due to insufficient study of the epoch, that the life went out of Spanish painting in the seventeenth century and that the first half of the eighteenth produced nothing of value, since it was only later that Goya triumphantly revived the native school. This is not the place to refute these erroneous assertions. It will be enough, perhaps, to indicate their falsity by a reference to the works of Luis Meléndez, born exactly thirty years before Goya, and in particular to the former's magnificent early portrait in the Louvre.

He painted many different subjects. But his individual style is best expressed in his still-life studies, by which he is chiefly known. As none of these appeared before 1762 we are bound to conclude, if the dates are reliable, that Meléndez did not turn to still-life before he had matured.

As a rule Spanish still-life painting is less notable for matter-of-fact representation of victuals and household utensils than for the immense pains taken by the artist to render the physical qualities of the objects depicted, as if he were positively in love with them. It is no wonder, therefore, that such pictures, for all their simplicity, exercise a profound fascination and are better understood and appreciated today than formerly.

The numerous works of Meléndez regularly prove his integrity as a craftsman and his thoughtful approach to the subject. No hurried or conventional passages can be detected. In each case he deliberately subordinates the total effect of the combined elements of his composition to that of a single fruit, fowl, tray of confectionery, slice of fish or piece of meat. In the canvas here considered a slice of salmon takes precedence. By this means he is able to unify and concentrate the visual impression. The technical rules of his day required the entire surface of a picture to be decorated, to the detriment of its illustrative quality, which Goya later restored even in his splendid still-life paintings.

This canvas, like all the other members of its series, was intended for the Aranjuez Palace, where there was a 'cabinet containing every variety of Spanish comestible'.

234

FRANCISCO DE GOYA *The Stilt-walkers*

FRANCISCO DE GOYA
*The Manikin ('El Pelele')*

FRANCISCO DE GOYA, 1746–1828 *The Wine-harvest*
Canvas: 108$^1$/$_4$ × 74$^3$/$_4$ in. (275 × 190 cm.) Cat. 795 (Reproduction p. 236)

Goya's productions for the Royal tapestry workshops are erroneously described as 'cartoons'. They were in fact canvases. A series entitled *The Four Seasons* is outstanding among them owing to its unity and intrinsic interest. In these works the artist went to nature for his inspiration and composed abstract allegories of the kind officially in favour. The four items of the series are *The Flower Girls, The Field, The Wine-harvest* and *Snow*. The first and the third, superior to the other two, go naturally together. Goya had at the time just been appointed, on 25 June 1786, Court Painter to Charles III. He seems to have determined, in the optimistic mood of that year, to paint his best.

No. 795 illustrates such aspects of Goya's genius as the delicacy and animation of his modelling of the features of women and children as well as his truth to nature, seen here both in his depiction of vine-leaves and grapes, and in his vivid rendering of the bright, luminous atmosphere in which his seven harvesters labour under the Castilian sky.

In certain passages, the skirts of the women for example, the reddish underpainting is visible through his thin glazes, so that an effect of solidity and realism is achieved. Such realistic effects in his work were not necessarily derived direct from nature. It is not therefore surprising to learn that, while the grape-harvest was being gathered in the near neighbourhood of the Court, Goya was punctual in his attendance at the

sessions of the Academy starting on 3 September of that year. This fact disposes of the conjecture that he may have been taking notes in the vineyards at this time.

The picture in question was commissioned from Goya to serve as a model for tapestry to be hung in the apartments of the Infante Gabriel, the translator of Sallust, and his wife Maria Anna Victoria, at the Escorial.

FRANCISCO DE GOYA, 1746–1828 *Doña Tadea Arias de Enríquez*
Canvas: 74³/₄ × 41³/₄ in. (190 × 106 cm.) Cat. 740

Nothing is known of the life of this handsome lady, whose coat of arms indicates that she was of noble birth, except that she was born about 1770 and married a man of rank named Enríquez. Goya, who enjoyed painting women's portraits and executed them admirably, produced most of his work in this field between 1785 and 1805. Charming feminine faces appear

FRANCISCO DE GOYA *The Family of Charles IV*

in his so-called 'cartoons' for the Royal tapestry workshop. Those entitled *Lady of Fashion and Harlequins, The Umbrella* and *Blindman's Buff* are especially memorable. But detached female portraits against a neutral background, undertaken purely for the sake of the sitter's physical attractions, begin only in the year 1786, with the portrait of the Marquesa de Pontejos now in the National Gallery, Washington.

The lack of extraneous elements in that portrait is still more noticeable in this one of Doña Tadea, where the garden setting is only suggested by a lightly sketched urn. Finally, in *La Tirana*, at the Academy of Fine Art, Madrid, and the wonderful *Condesa del Carpio,* in the Louvre, nothing whatever distracts attention from the subject.

According to the Count of Viñaza the portrait of Doña Tadea was purchased from Goya in 1793 or 1794. It seems strange that a writer with documents at his disposal should be uncertain of the exact date. But the invoice appears to indicate a somewhat earlier period and it has therefore been supposed that the portrait was painted prior to the long illness of the artist which began at the end of 1792 and that payment was delayed. This hypothesis would account for the lack of precise information.

In the portrait of Doña Tadea, Goya employs the method referred to in my note on No. 795, using the reddish first coat to obtain extremely delicate effects of transparency with thinly applied white tones, thrown into relief by the black of the voluminous gauze bow.

This painting is of so exquisite a quality that it stays in the memory as one of the finest of all time, owing to the contrast of the almost childish features of the model with a coquettish sophistication in the gesture with which she draws on her glove.

F<small>RANCISCO DE</small> G<small>OYA</small>, 1746–1828 *The Painter Francisco Bayeu*
Canvas: 44¹/₈ × 33¹/₈ in. (112 × 84 cm.) Cat. 721

This portrait is the most elegant and lively of those painted by Goya of men during the eighteenth century. It challenges comparison with contemporary portraits of the English School, among which few can rival its brilliance. Goya reveals the psychology of his sitter to an extent which other artists of the day rarely contrived.

Francisco Bayeu was born at Saragossa in 1734 and died at Madrid on 4 August 1795. He himself and two of his brothers were painters; Goya married his sister, but the two artists had been associated prior to this union, for in 1770 Goya, while in Italy, declared himself a pupil of Bayeu, though no proof has come to light of such a connection. Bayeu was official painter to the King and therefore in a position to use his influence on Goya's behalf. But relations between the two men were often strained, especially in 1771, while Goya was painting frescoes in the Pilar Cathedral at Saragossa. In the course of time, however, and with the coming of success, these misunderstandings were forgotten.

It was in 1786 that Goya first painted his brother-in-law's portrait. This admirable work is preserved at the Valencia Gallery. The portrait here under consideration was executed after Bayeu's death, in grey tones of great subtlety. It was doubtless modelled on Bayeu's self-portrait, then in the possession of the Marques de Toca. Some weeks after the death of Francisco Bayeu the portrait in grey was sent by Goya to the exhibition held by the San Fernando Academy of Fine Art. The catalogue states that it was then unfinished. But it must have been completed later, for no fault can now be found with its first-rate technical accomplishment.

Goya succeeded Bayeu as Director of Painting at the Academy, but the latter's works are unremarkable and have contributed less to his fame than the two superb portraits bequeathed to posterity by his brother-in-law.

FRANCISCO DE GOYA
*Portrait of Doña Maria Josefa*

FRANCISCO DE GOYA
*Portrait of the Infante
Don Francisco de Paula Antonio*

FRANCISCO DE GOYA *The Maja Nude*    FRANCISCO DE GOYA *The Maja Clothed*

FRANCISCO DE GOYA, 1746–1828 *Ferdinand VII wearing the Royal Cloak*
Canvas: 83¹/₂ × 57¹/₂ in. (212 × 146 cm.) Cat. 735 (Reproduction p. 242)

Even though the King is wearing the Royal Cloak as well as the Order of
the Golden Fleece and that of Charles III – ceremonial attire unusual in the
portraits of the Spanish monarchs, who tended to dress unostentatiously –
an element of caricature is apparent in the King's features. It shows how
little admiration and affection the Court Painter had for Ferdinand, who,
however, compensated for his errors by creating the Prado museum.

There is another portrait in existence which is similar in spite of a slight
difference in size. This is also in the Prado and here the King is represented
in an encampment with horses, soldiers and tents.

In these two paintings Goya, Chief Court Painter, fulfils his duty as
portrait painter of the 'awaited King' who is returning from exile. Already
in the canvas that we have reproduced here, the feeling of distance is apparent.

Whereas Velasquez tried to give noble dignity to everyone who posed
for him – children, princes and dwarves, princesses and buffoons – purely
for the pleasure of making them noble and beautiful, it seems that the
artist from Aragon applied his critical powers to the models he did not
like, such as royal personages and those on a somewhat higher level of
society. On the other hand he reserved all the richness of his style to
magnify the beauty and elegance of those models who impressed him
favourably (the Marchioness of Pontejos, the Duchess of Alba, the Countess
of Chinchon, Doña Isabel Colos de Porcel, the Duchess of Osuna, Doña
Tadea Arias de Enríquez . . .).

Goya's satirical streak showed itself most keenly when he was painting
members of the Royal Family. Of the dozen or so members of Charles IV's
family who posed for him, only the young Infante Don Francisco de Paula
Antonio escapes the severe criticism of the artist. It is more apparent in
the portraits of Charles IV, Marie-Louise and Ferdinand VII.

Because of his title of Court Painter Goya still seems to have kept his satirical attitude but his latent aggressiveness was projected into his etchings and black paintings.

At the request of the Academy Goya painted a portrait of Ferdinand VII on horseback shortly after Ferdinand's accession to the throne.

After this he painted other royal portraits for Pampelone (Pamplona?), Santander and Saragossa.

FRANCISCO DE GOYA, 1746–1828 *The Colossus (Panic)*
Canvas: 45⅝ × 41⅜ in. (116 × 105 cm.) Cat. 2785

Goya's work in the set of etchings known as *Los Caprichos,* published
in 1779, borders on the fantastic. But a humorous or sarcastic intention
underlies the fantasy, at times deliberately terrifying. It is only, however,
in two of the *Caprichos* (Nos. 3 and 52) that he introduces a figure of

243

enormous size with a view to this latter effect, though some years later forms of at any rate gigantic proportions appear in the *Proverbios* and *Disparates* ('Extravagances') series.

I believe that the canvas here reproduced dates from a period intermediary between those of the *Caprichos* and *Disparates* and was probably executed about the same time as the unique etching also called *The Colossus,* though there is no visible relation between the two. We are here more likely to be concerned with the picture entitled *The Giant* in the inventory of Goya's possessions drawn up in 1812.

It represents the flight of human beings and cattle from a huge and dreadful apparition which rises through clouds above a range of mountains. This subject carries allusions to actual events, for the dispersion illustrated is centrifugal, radiating from a motionless creature indifferent to what is going on all round it. The fantastic colossus may be a symbol for Napoleon, for panic in general or simply for the approach of an epidemic. I feel myself that the implication suggested by the creature and its attitude is political.

These various alternative interpretations of the actual meaning of the subject make no difference to its stirring impact, due to the violent, one might almost say furious, execution of the work. Some passages have been laid on with the palette-knife. Others, in contrast, owe their vibrant quality to brief, rapid strokes of the brush.

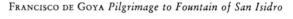

FRANCISCO DE GOYA *Pilgrimage to Fountain of San Isidro*

FRANCISCO DE GOYA *The Fates*

FRANCISCO DE GOYA *The Witches' Sabbath*

FRANCISCO DE GOYA, 1746–1828 *Saturn devouring one of his Children*
Mural transferred to canvas: $57^{1}/_{8} \times 32^{5}/_{8}$ in. (146 × 83 cm.) Cat. 763
(Reproduction p. 246)

It seems inexplicable that Goya should have painted this terrifying
scene to decorate, in common with his *Judith*, the dining-room on the
ground floor of his country villa. The artist, then in his seventies, was
a prey to the 'dreams' he had illustrated forty years previously in the
*Caprichos*.

Neither the extraordinary precedent of a picture by Rubens in the
possession of the Prado nor the bitter humour of the grimace of time
swallowing up its days can alleviate the appalling character of this production. But to conquer one's disgust and contemplate the painting as a work
of art is to be confounded by its amazing forecast of expressionism.

245

It may, however, be observed, with regard to the series of frescoes at Goya's villa known as his 'black paintings', that their dominant chiaroscuro is in fact relieved by other tones.

246

FRANCISCO DE GOYA *The Second of May, 1808*    FRANCISCO DE GOYA *The Third of May, 1808*

FRANCISCO DE GOYA, 1746–1828 *The Milkmaid of Bordeaux*
Canvas: 29¹/₈ × 26³/₄ in. (74 × 68 cm.) Cat. 2899 (Reproduction p. 248)

One of Goya's last paintings and his final tribute to the 'eternal feminine' principle which played so essential a part in his inspiration, the *Milkmaid* represents the spirited figure which arrived on donkey-back every morning at No. 39, Cours de l'Intendance, where the painter lived and was soon to die.

As is well known Goya, who had never been precocious, improved his technical skill to a prodigious degree in old age. With justified pride he added the words 'eighty-one years old' to his signature on the portrait of his friend Muguiro, now in the Prado. Modern criticism finds the portrait in question fifty years ahead of its time. The technique of the *Milkmaid* is even more advanced, for in this case the juxtaposition of brief strokes of different colours seems to anticipate 'divisionism'. But these almost incredible technical innovations were employed to express the psychology of the painter's models, which he penetrated at least as deeply in these works as in those of his maturity. The new methods were not devised to disguise the effects of failing sight or manual dexterity. They were the result of a deliberate search for suitable means of recording the artist's sensibility. It is impossible to avoid wondering what developments in his work would have ensued if, instead of dying at eighty-two, he had lived to be a hundred, as Titian is said to have done.

Doña Leocadia Zorrilla, a strange woman who had led an extraordinary life and was Goya's companion at Bordeaux, offered this picture, on 9 December 1829, to Juan Muguiro, the painter's friend mentioned above. She told him that her distressed circumstances obliged her to sell it but that Goya had warned her not to part with it for less than an *onza*, a Spanish gold coin worth about four pounds.

The Count of Muguiro bequeathed this admirable painting to the Prado in 1946.

FRANCISCO DE GOYA *Self-Portrait*

FRANCISCO DE GOYA *Two women laughing*

FRANCISCO DE GOYA *A Manola*

# LIST OF ILLUSTRATIONS

The numbers in italics denote colour plates

# INDEX

# THE ARRANGEMENT OF THE MUSEUM

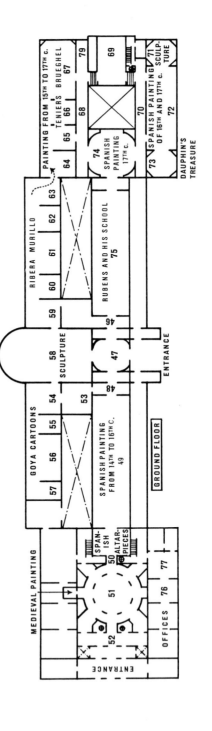

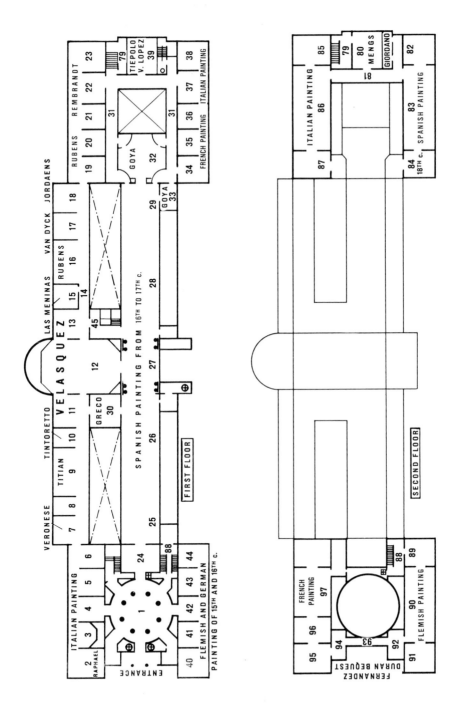